RELICS AND FANCIES

of

ZEBULON MACSWINE

RELICS AND FANCIES

of

ZEBULON MACSWINE

by

DEREK COLVILLE

British Library Cataloguing-in-Publication Data.

A catalogue record for this book is
available from the British Library.

ISBN 0–9523131–0–3

Typeset by Create Publishing Services Limited, Bath, Avon.
Printed and bound by The Looseleaf Company, Melksham, Wiltshire.

SANEVERSE
100, Austin Fields
King's Lynn
Norfolk PE30 1RS

Cry

God, how has it come about,
That she, once, entering a room,
Lit up the sun:
Now, years gone,
Taking revenge, the sun
Illumes the universe
Once she's gone out?

"I also know," said Candide, "that we must go and work in the garden."

Zebulon,
Being sixty-nine,
Wrote down
What stuck in the head
Of life gone.
Shame, that worthier,
Weightier things, have fled;
While stuff of fools
Survives; but that's
The way the game is,
Not the rules.
Not poems, these,
Pieces.
What they speak of
Was his.

NINETEEN TWENTIES

1 First Sociology Lesson

I see the legs, that belonged to me,
Push towards neat-turned bed sheets:
Ankles, small silky socks; patent shoes, buttoning across.
I pulled them back; two years of living said: know,
Shoes into sheets don't go.

It's all right: Put them in, Love,
Said my Grandma (words since longed
To be heard again).
And I did – put them right down in the bed.
She was in bed all the time (heart, they said)
And had some money. Even fools
Would know: that changed the rules.

2   Dramatics

The play was *Canute*, and they told me to be
As the youngest (and only boy), the sea.
I had a blue cloth which, under, was black.
And the King, the star, couldn't turn me back.

They laughed, and still do, at the part I played.
It did make your arms tired, making waves;
But under the cloth they couldn't see.
It still seems to me the place to be.

3 Milk Mornings

At ten thirty – precisely – we filed out for our milk
At Moseley's Dairy; and the smell I've searched for
Sixty years, and never come near. What was it? Butter,
Cream, cleanness? Girls with breasts and fullness
Behind the counter, who smiled, and were warm?
I was nearly five, and unsure.

The only boy. And what was strange,
I knew – I knew – that if I just stood there
A kind of love enveloped, wrapped me round, from the
     light of smiles,
Undemanding, freely advanced, given.

I could cause that, could make it happen, without trying.
Then I changed schools: no more milk mornings.
I searched, longed, almost found it again;
Almost made it happen
Fifty times – sixty, seventy over the years,
But never quite.

It snowed, blew, and cut. All was pain,
Pain everything. The head longs to flee,
But there's nowhere to run.
The ice makes you slip, and it's dark.
As huge grey shapes pass, indifferently,
Can't they see, how much it hurts,
What it's like to be me?

The butcher's boy sees me; gives chase on his bike,
For I wear a grey cap with a star on top, meaning
Mrs. Gilbey's School – proper name: All Saints
(Private: two guineas a term).

I run, slip, and run. He catches me;
His nose a red bulb, and drops twinkling
Over the clouds of breath, the slack-open mouth,
Eyes above small in delight.
His mate holds me down: he paints my face blue,
And lets me go (worse shame – can't I say I broke free?)
The wind and the shivering again ate up me;
The journey towards home, nearly a mile,
Sobbing, slobbering-wet, no better than his nose,
Than his lips. The longest, longest ever mile,
Further than the end of pain.

So I learned about where I lived,
And the class system.
How can you grow up in a mile?

A bit rougher, this school, but money-free.
And there was Miss C,
Tall, fair, hair rolled round the edges,
Distant to all, but kind to me.

It was all there in the smile,
Correct, just pleasant, seen superficially;
But I knew, certain, it beamed a sort of love
(No better, or different, a word) for me.

All knowledge, one moment, imprisoned in a child.
No better than old age;
The same knowing, in body old.
Neither can reply.

One day I slipped, fell on the playground slope;
No pain at all, but blood-drip, drip from somewhere.
Led (all pity) into the school, mistresses fussy, sorry-
  solicitous
(Presaging, some future longing pang?)

And the eyes, as we walked: shocked,
Sensation-loving, greedy, impressed;
As the blood dripped, steadily,
First on gravel, then wood, then carpet.

Then unremembered stitchings, a journey, must have
  been;
No memory of all that; still no pain.

Now, one lifetime after, just a chin-scar, still
With playground gravel-bits in it.
And in the mind, the pleasure of the stir, fame-like,
And, always, the eyes.

NINETEEN THIRTIES

Turn up tomorrow, ten o'clock they said,
Here's your shirt. You're left back.
So I did, and looked exactly
Like a little footballer.
Knowing no rules, trying to look like others,
Trying not to be where the ball was
(It wouldn't stay away),
Trying to find the right stance,
So as not to be noticed;
A small blue-shirted footballer
Knowing not one rule,
Playing for Gladstone Road School.

The others knew, knew what to do;
Had learned in the streets, with others,
And had been told.
But I, from private school,
Had no play-streets, no others.
You're left back, they said, turning away.
How did I know then I was a right wing?
Why didn't I know about football then,
And do, now I'm old?

Friday was sums day, nine to ten.
Some, the terrified, were at school by seven,
Some earlier (you could start on arrival).
Eight sums: how long the long division then!
Pop Watt came round, as you worked them out,
Shouting only when temper broke, intent,
Watching my hand, writing. He smelt of his life,
Like most, a bit bad, indefinable, sour snout,
The nose pink, strawberry, with holes, the hairs
Sticking from it; hard breaths over your shoulder, but
   controlled.

He was back by eleven, all papers marked,
Haranguing his way through the sums, rising to shouts
At crucial points, and fools who'd got it wrong.
For each sum wrong, one stroke with thick hard stick,
Like a top-whip stick; what hurt on were the bones.
Once, Zebulon's stick-score was five, with blue-bruised
   thumbs.
No comment. Think what you like: grown, and at science,
   thick,
He's slick and right at sums.

9   Impasse

In ninety-thirty-three, there was a show,
Scientific, at the Spa, by the sea:
A robot gleaming, all knobs and wires,
Proportioned as a man, but huge,
Forerunner of the future age.
His master, half magician, made –
Forced – Zeb to come upon the stage
To question It, claiming
That it would answer – answer anything.
When he arrived up there, the lad, unwillingly
Torn from his anonymity,
Bared, unprotected; most shy, far
Beyond the fearing, could not move
Nor blurt a single word, express
Anything. He stood: the minutes ticked, he in distress.
Heart pounds; face flushed,
All motionless; with every eye –
Of crowd, master and metal monster
Upon him: more time passed;
More, and then – more yet.
The Thing, seeming to know,
Raised gleaming arms, turned helmet-head;
Appeared to grin,
Performing its set motions.
Master, betrayed, seeming a sham,
Angry: the audience laughed.
The boy, who caused all this, by nothing,
Sneaked off, ashamed.

13

From where does he,
A boy, acquire
A sensibility?
At eleven to twelve,
The new school (prize
Of scholarship success)
Overwhelms.
Zeb dreams: he is
No more than slightly there,
Though physically, Present, Sir.
"A moderate record
Of moderate effort here,"
Says his report:
(Assessment you might well apply
To his subsequent career).

Then, a strange day, he found himself
Running, with older lads, trance-like,
In the cross-country race, imposed
Each year, slept through at half-trot
By most. But these lads, at the front
Somehow with Zeb, they wore school running vests,
Red bands around their middles;
All trained, hardened, representatives, famed
Locally; they smiled, because of the intruder,
But only at each other.
He held on, driven by a kind of fear,
Then some new iron in the will;
A mystery, sudden-there.
Others dropped away,
Till at the end, the hills
And miles gone,
There were three, only:
Zeb and two, left.

A desperate sprint between
The crowd, as they jostled, tore
Down: Zeb second, by six inches,
To a winner of eighteen (record time),
Long dead now, since the war.

From that day, all was changed.
He was there; body, head as well.
Shaped, too, somehow come home
By Harry Wharton, and the rest,
The Famous Five, *Magnet*
And *Gem*: which is not
A bad way to become.

How could it be so – always summer,
Always sun-evenings? Zeb, alone, house his own;
The bookcase, tall, near-threatening, full of past:
Volumes of Dickens (illus.), and the musty smell
Of mysteries, gone and remote.
Upstairs, in the huge drawer-chest,
Yesterday things: jewels, caskets padded, scarves,
Fans, ivory, and jet;
All with the strange, elusive, almost
Religious scent, even yet.

Was it these things
Or solitude (the friend
Scarce introduced),
Knowledge of being young, with all to come,
Sunset, or some alchemy
Of all of these, that made
Once, and more than once
The most delirious-mad, drunken
Joy, that would not stay within the limbs,
Jumping, leaping, bounding for outlet,
The most stupendous, crazed
Half-painful joy
Then, or yet.

First, the tiny, perfect blonde girl
(Seen decades later wheeling a pram,
Smiling the memory-smile)
Came round, to catch young Zeb
In evening, as he hit a tennis ball
Against house-wall.
He, astonished, overwhelmed
To find his world invaded,
And by the force of what he wished,
Could not receive it into the flats of life,
And ran.

Next, the peach-flushed beauty, gold-pink, blue-eyed,
So *everything* then, family-guarded,
Remote, in hiatus
Cut off from all approach,
Who, in some forfeit game within the dark
Placed Zeb's hand there.
Yes, there, on the rustling silk
And paralysed him.

And last in series,
The girl more earthy,
Also lovely: she who moved
With grace; head tilted high, hair shining,
Swinging as she walked.
This time he reached,
Found, and was caught;
Part of him ever.

What was it, from this,
That gripped him a lifetime?
Forcing the pattern, quest and seeking, never ending,
Over, over again, over yet.

So far as he can see, beating the brain,
It was the hair, or,
Beyond, deeper than that
The lovely contradiction, never
Explained, never made captive,
Between the groped pubic wires
And the bright softness swinging round the head.
Let him explore, explore –
Seeking his core.

The train from Malton
Was empty of people
And full, full of sun.
No corridor: he was alone.

He had just won his town the race,
As Housman said;
And was fifteen.

All you do
Is push, inside, inside of body,
Inside of everything.
The legs sweep you through,
Easily, as you watch the others
Pass away, behind,
Effortlessly.

Exultation is made of Future.
He knew, as he looked in the mirror
Between the adverts, all sun-lit, all golden-gold,
That he couldn't keep the thrill-gold,
The beauty, inside.

Is happiness an itch behind the chest,
Surging, consuming, spilling over?
Nineteen miles, alone, of ecstasy;
He thought of the endless future to spend, carelessly;
Knowing, simultaneously, this was the highest,
Not quite to return
Ever.
And so it has been.

It was the Cup.
Eleven thousand, more, a quarter of the town
Packed close.
Young Zeb, with father, grateful to be taken,
Pressing the fence, up hard
Against the wood that pushed back on his chest;
Ground-level, not best for seeing.
The Boro, beloved, as now,
From minor league (Midland)
Against Luton Town, from (yes, it was true)
The proper Football League,
Division Two.

It went much as you'd think:
An early goal for them, gods
In white silk shirts. No chance
Of even denting them. But we did:
A penalty.

The boy, hemmed in – paralysed, amazed;
Amazing hope; no room for other,
Saw the brown ball, thwack, hit the net, shake the cord,
Mere feet away, and could not take it in,
Never believe. But it was so:
One-all, and in the end a draw.
Newspapers said so too.
And though he himself never heard it confirmed there,
It must have been, on the wireless.

From the stand now, comfortable,
With (alas!) a sense of proportion,
I see him there, and always
When the Boro take a corner
Close to the spot

20

(Never when opponents do – why not?);
A different fence, with adverts now, but
Same earth – at least deep down –
On it, the boy, standing
Frozen, numb-tense,
Then with joy, exulting, then
Only half-believing.
Strange to me, now, inside this head,
He looking the same, but a stranger, never met,
Not face to face.
No father is with him;
Where has his father gone?

If I got up, left this comfortable seat
And roof against the rain,
Walking around, to the Seamer Road end,
To see him closer, ask him
Where his father was,
Near the goal where
We equalised, in
Nineteen-thirty-eight,
There would be only air.

A few, the weaker ones, were absent-ill
For half-days: terror had won.
He had fame; was a myth
Of the town, and beyond, well beyond.
Herr Bonn: pronounced in quiet; no need
To speak loudly of torment, not if it touched you;
But said with a remoter awe,
Half gratitude, if your life was not affected
By what you spoke of. "Air Bon,"
They'd say, and tell one of the stories.
Air Bon: echoing, echoing yet,
Herr Bonn: purest terror, essence, thing itself;
First rumoured, something on the air, then known
In lonely fears, then met.

The day came: expectation, fears planted, rise;
Tension steady, then electric. We sat silent, trapped:
The door moved. He stood,
Famous, the one famous man we knew:
Famous, now here; now, now.
Grey suit, waistcoat, ordinary enough,
But the trousers strange, narrow,
Descending to large shoes, with soles
Thick, enormous, like no others seen by boys.
Face, not irregular; though somehow, even when still,
Bringing to mind a snorting horse.
The mouth strong, barely contained;
The nose hairs (why do they all
Have those?); browned skin, a few freckles,
A little reddish hair; eyes small
So far as could be discerned,
For you could never dare to look
Directly. Movements precise, military:
He knew what was created, knew

Where he had us.
So we sat doomed, in mathematic rows
Precisely fixed, thirty or so in ranks by skill
And favour: the Good at front,
Hopeless in rear.
Zeb, newly transferred to this (O Luck, O Pity),
Was twenty-sixth: as week-years passed,
He rose a bit; to midst,
Which was his natural home;
Once, to fifth.

Roll first: *"Hier, Herr Starke."*
He had, amazingly, a proper name (and Starke?),
Even a Christian one: Erskine.
How could that be?
Then, The Test. We'd had to learn
From his own grammar book
Exemplary German sentences.
The grammar's points, behind them, could be
Safely ignored, being outside The Test.
So Zeb, now old, when German touristing
Can still say, perfectly:
"Es ist nützlich, schwimmen zu können,"
And it is useful to be able to swim,
Though not so much in the street.
Aeons ago, he wrote it well enough;
Always four sentences of the twenty learned
The night before. Change papers;
Then the scores: *Vier, Herr Starke;*
Zwei, Eins, Herr Starke;
Suitable looks distributed, as he wrote:
Small quarter-loosenings of the mouth
For favourites, scoring four;
Scowl, sigh, hesitation, half a threat
To come at them, the others, bodily.
Most dreaded, next, the staple of the day's

23

Routine: reading, translating Turns.
Starting at front, all smooth, correct,
Received almost affectionately,
All of us smiling – even the back rows – dutifully.
Wild hopes begin to stir
That this might last, could last
(For it was even said
That one or two of these bright favoured ones
Went, at weekends, to his house for tea
And table-tennis).
It did not last; favourites done,
The unknown thing, feared, hanging in air, began:
Towards the middle rows – always there,
Always: (there was a hopeless, shrugged
Half-pity for idiot back ones, not often
Reached). But the middle – them!
There lay, in wait, the essence of it all,
The source of myth – myth not known of
(So ran professional pretence)
By any other teacher in the school.
Here it comes, now: the slight flush, the brutal
Tightening of the mouth, wetting of the lips,
The relish, chewed, savoured: "Ah now, Master G.,"
(His name was Gregory)
"O well, we might as well, all of us,
Suffer your usual performance.
Get on." ... "*Der Mann ist –*"
"That's enough, Lad." (No friendly "lad," that,
The razor-blade one). "As you know
Perfectly well, Gregory" (the name, said grinding
With the teeth, as dogs, savaging),
"It is not *Der Mann*.
It is *Der Mann*. Say it, properly."
So it was said, by each, indistinguishably
In sound, by each, some hundred times,
Volleying, perpetual grim tennis,

24

Back and forth, the menace
Rising each stroke, the fury in the air,
Each voice nearer to breaking
In its own way, each one
Of a hundred, mounting steps;
The stealthy, quiet move
On the thick soles, to the boy's desk:
"Why d'you do it, Lad, WHY, every time?
Just tell us." "Well Sir –"
A hundred Well Sirs, and Just Tell Us,
Varied by Simply Tell Us;
A hundred interruptions, each
More soaked in menace, till
The explosion of the fist on desk
Expected yet still shattering; an inch
Or two from the boy's face.
(He never touched you: that was well known;
Even when given over to fury, utterly;
Never: the rumour was, that once
He had done, wounding; but if so, the thing
Whatever it had been, lay buried
In dead past.) We thought of that
Until the second crash, louder yet,
Split the summer, outside,
And Gregory, punch-drunk, pale, just flesh, no more,
Surrendered. "I Was Careless,
Sir." "Why didn't you say so?
Well Lad, now you've wasted all our time
With that performance" – huge turnip watch
Produced from waistcoat – "we may as well
Shut up shop for the day, and come back
At four o'clock." So we did; so it went. And after,
You lived a normal life until next time
Loomed, the tight dread gathered, usually –
Time being what it is while young –
The day before. They said – but myths

25

Do father yet more rumour – that he admired
Hitler, just over there: maybe; Zeb doubted that, and
Even more, that Hitler would have done the same
For him.
Once, he kept Zeb back,
After school, keeping him
From a mile race. There was protest,
Official – headmaster, sports master, others.*
And he apologised – said the words
And in class. Zeb admired that; but
On the whole he'd have preferred
Him to remain himself, consistently.
Can we cling, even, to terror that we know
Hating alteration?

What was the Thing
He made, creeping
Closer through the air,
To make the stomach lurch, heart thump
In echoing thump, throat dry, robbed
Of swallowing? We're glib
With the terms, now: psychology
Of terror; and the rest. Zeb cannot know.
But, three times a week
Eternally, it was there, its taste
In mouth, blood, veins,
Seizing the muscles. Enough remains
To fend off half a century, living on.

Of twenty teaching
In the decent, sunny school,
There was one other:
Lean, tall, jaundice-yellow;
Black moustache, brutal
But an ordinary sadist
With a gymshoe;
Always curdled;
Compressed fury behind
The words: berserk only when
Aroused, gymshoes on rumps,
To ecstasy.

Nothing special, though;
Run of the mill.
Not in Bonn's class;
Becoming a magistrate,
Much respected.

17 Young Zeb's Irish Poem
(Made in School)

Does *Ire*-land mean *Anger*-land?
Because, for six, eight centuries
(Give or take), the English pillaged sore,
And harried there. (I'm not too sure
What harrying is.)

Well, in the end, they went back
To *status quo*, just as they ought.
Stopped hanging, shooting, pillaging
(And all that harrying),
And made things right – gave the place
Back to the Irish: cleared out
In nineteen-twenty-one. (Go always to first
Causes, then correct them; so would say
Our history master, Mr. McNay.
He's a B.A.)

But they did keep the Northern bit
Where they'd planted Scots-Prots, before.
The shooting, killing (and harrying)
Still go on there; a sort of steady war
In every decade, and for all of it.

The big nobs here, from P.M. down
To Ministers, and M.s of P.
(There's scores of them – they seem
To change so frequently –
Parading, preening, always on stage),
Yet the performance stays the same;
All say the same:–
"... Appalled ... Outraged ... Disgusted
At inhuman acts, by terrorist scum"
(That means the other side, the I.R.A.)

"And this above all: we'll never, never,
Never give way."
The trouble is, though they could give
The Northern bit back too, and gradually
By timetable, most Scots-Prots
Want to stay
In the U.K.,
Land of O.K.
And Give Away.
My dad says that his taxes pay.
(I'm sure, not just his –
It's only Social Just His.)

If they did give the North bit back,
At least some Scots-Prots, they would stay
On, and be Irish. They know that Prots
Down in Eire, they're treated O.K.

But others would insist they stay
In the U.K. Since there was pay
To plant them in (back to the start again
Says Mr. McNay), you'd have to say
To all those old-time plants:– Come
To England, just like all others welcomed in.
Please accept, and be transplanted.
Do come. Be Resettelment (Sp?) Granted.

But where's the cash
To come from?
Well, from what they'd no more have to pay
To keep the Army there for years,
Just to referee the killing.
Pack all that in: use the Queen's shilling
To make Prots far, far more than willing
To leave.

Mr. McNay, who's a B.A.,

And teaches history,
Gave me eight out of ten
For this essay;
And he added that, one day,
P.M.s, Ministers, and M.s of P.
Might even (nearly, anyway)
Catch up to me.

H. McN.

$^{8}/_{10}$

Promising. But do not overdo parentheses.

NINETEEN FORTIES

The rhythm of the Thirties was trochaic;
Unsettling, jagged; shot with pain, and fear of it.
The ugly, the marching poor;
The Bright, pro-Red, escaping it.
Always threat, gathering,
Lowering clouds, the false alarms
Postponing final moments, final death
That cost the marching everyone in arms
Their everything, breath.

So they said. But to young Zeb
It was never so. His years then
Were endless moments, blue and gold
Shining, all in place. A thousand old
Tiny moments, generating (more where they
Came from) limitless into future, impelling
The heart to lurch with joy,
With the promise of it, promise, always promising,
He being young.

Wrong, it seems now, he was.
Full of illusion – no more than juice
To push the years on, making it all
For a while, worthwhile. It seems
So, now.
And yet, once, the boy
Stood above the beach, and knew,
Beyond the logic of the wire, tank traps and such,
They would not come. It would not do.
The lovely sameness of the years, a trace of that
Was there, still.
Nothing now so ill, no myth of might
Could become, to mar that. So thought the young fool.
And he was right.

War now, supposed to alter all
(And did, in the end) altered nothing yet.
So Zeb, lording it in his school-world,
Bright, newly bright, and athlete, lionised,
A Harry Wharton, modest, boy-fiction realised,
Left, before his time; McCrea and windmills in his head
And aeroplanes. Embryo foreign correspondent as
He saw himself, though never said.

Truth is always other.
The *Daily Mirror*, Manchester: small concrete
Block of offices, off Deansgate, and a city.
Strange, afraid, Zeb; nothing to thrill on being
Loose in real life, the thing itself, no longer
Having to dream of it. Digs
In Northenden, and kindly. Thank you
Bill Skinner, technician printer and his wife.
But the rest of it! Office, full of well
Greased, shiny, large-portly-prosperous
Outgoers, the power of the press.
All beer and boast. On the make,
Self-delighted, luxurious, expense-wizards.
(Quite some way from the Famous Five.)
Here, daily prospering jousts in self-love, twisting,
    worming;
Expense-inventiveness and brag, each
Skilled to insinuate and crawl. The object at the top
As president, was Arvin P.,
Grey, sixties and remote, a leech,
To take in every unctuous drop of soul,
Drawing, collecting, swallowing, seeming never
To eat, but to imbibe, without the swelling.
A distant emperor, upstairs, speaking directly
Only to London.

With a first minister: what was
He – news editor, chief sub-editor?
Something. It mattered more that he
(It was well-known, he saw to that)
Had been to grammar school,
Matriculated. A festering superiority
Lived in the neat small head,
The plastered hair. What's left of him?
For Zeb, only the memory of an exchange
By hated 'phone: Zeb quoting, and truly,
An old girl, bombed out, who had said,
"Till ...." Small Plastered Head,
Coldly, the knowledge-voice,
"There's no such word." And Zeb,
At seventeen, dutifully said "Until,"
As required. What would he give, now,
To unsay the surrender, to have said instead,
"There bloody well is, you supercilious
Bastard, and that's what she said."

This the adventure world
Of press. He did learn misery;
To stay apart, quiet, nursing the schoolboy past:
To send pictures, telephoto, to type one finger, fast;
Longing to cry on secretaries' shoulders, for they at least
Were girls. He learned to write
Mindless, *Mirror*-stuff (easy), and not be
Too ashamed (impossible, quite).

Not his father's Manchester, warm-remembered,
Warmly told. What else of it? A flat
Of his own, in Sale, and that
One monster room, of space and Thirties chrome,
Run by two luscious twins, blonde, always at home.
And when Zeb, posted away
Said his goodbye, late in the day,

They were in bed. Odd, he thought then;
Inviting, now. Being full of woe,
Misery-alone, he shook hands (hands!)
Correctly, and left
For Middlesbro.

No friend. One half-friend, Graham.
His surname, that (first name not now known);
Placed much the same, but capable;
Less shocked, resilient, less horrified;
Seeming all balance, more his own man than Zeb;
Knew how to put up with things, unsurprised.
Horatio, untainted: one who could cope;
But not with the war, which killed him
In some way Zeb desires not to know,
Shortly after; soon gone.

The *Daily Mirror* Regiment (14th Creepers)
Had its Home Guard.
Zeb, dressed like a soldier,
Must have drilled, over and over,
Hard, forgotten military poses,
All to commands. All dead now.
One moment only, survives;
One moment: there he stands
In the concrete entrance – just a doorway;
Some moon; night clear; sky black,
Sprinkled with stars; four a.m. Zeb leans back,
Lee-Enfield paining the shoulder on its strap;
Alone, in all the little street; beyond,
All Deansgate, still; all the might
Of Manchester – so it feels to him,
All on his back. What shall he do
(He in charge of a whole war, not happened yet)
If he should sudden sight
The parachutes' floating silent silhouettes
Against the moon, as in his hundred dreams
At school? Swing his gun down
And fire? Steadfastly? In panic?
Or will he run, clattering the gun away?
Do nothing, freeze?
All stayed still. He never knew
How there could be such lack of life, of sounds,
Of answers: except he knows, now
(Not thought of, then)
His rifle had no rounds.

I will tell you: you cannot know
What it was like in winter, nineteen-forty,
In Middlesbro.
Setting: – Zeb's aspidistra digs; pince-nez
Landlady, distant in old decades, not known.
Terraces, grime-flat, corroded, coughs
Of Thirties pain (not his father's place
Of flesh-escape, now all worked off).
Is Zeb a seventeen-year-aged ghost,
Travelling his father's tracks, not grown
Enough, to report decay? Nothing to report;
Nothing, nothing. No story-bits to 'phone,
No happenings. One spark
Once a day, when
The Gazette came out. But nothing there
For Zeb. How do you do this job, in space
Of nothing, withering, with not a bomb, no 'plane
Ever near the place?

If the Saturday was right,
He could forget, have sausages and chips
At Binns' Café, and see the Boro play;
Yet, the wrong Boro
By fifty miles, and a world away,
And Zeb On Duty.

An afternoon: he, desperate,
Went to the Odeon, seeing it round
More than twice. A friendly one, bespectacled,
Gentle-seeming, spoke (Zeb's first word
From a native), walked him back
And, back to wall, pinioned Zeb within his arms.
Panic could deal with it. Panic broke the grip,
Panic ran. Even the wrong sort of sex

Had to conform, then, to the law
Of nothing. And girls, not anywhere, and not
For him. Nothing in the aspidistra digs, or out.
Nothing weeks, piling up to doom.
He broke, telling no one, not the hated 'phone;
Shrugged his first adult shrug;
Went home.

They rang him after three weeks. He,
Glad to be sacked, prepared some
Insolence, at last. Even that
Was thwarted, for the Emperor,
Mindful, careful of some distant chance
Of influence (Zeb's cousin at London office?),
Words meticulously selected,
Merely consigned him to Hull, where
Raids were expected.

This was different, full
Of alive things. Zeb's digs
For instance. Landlady, Ede,
Bosom-warm, red-cheeked,
Laughing, half-mother, half sex-
Aware, and pleased, always pleased to be
Laughing there, with him. Dear Ede!
With the mean-dried, sour-drawn husband.
She tried to give to Zeb her niece –
Push, manage, encourage – but she, quiet,
Nice girl well-formed, was sallow,
Ill-complexioned. Zeb, starved as you were,
Why so particular?

They were right, at last, about the raids –
Those nights, with Ede, beneath the stairs
In the small cupboard, flinching
Yet laughing, all new-male reassurance, comfort
Unskilfully put on. After each whine,
Each crash, the dazed doubt, the elation,
Relief, then bravado, immortality
He thought. When the light came,
Out, self-importantly, to report:
Whole terraces, packs of mean houses

40

Gone, but not cleared; all dust,
Rubbish, old bricks. There were
Theatre sets, intimate rooms, opened
Cross-sections, chairs in place, pictures
Still on walls, aslant in the dust.
Officials, swelled, in charge, dictating
Imperatives: must this, must that;
Ropes, helmets, police, ARP-ers; groups gossiping;
Death coming down to rumour-chat.
A word or two with some old soul,
And there's a *Mirror* story
Full of tears, ignorance, and patriotic guts:
She seeks her cat, which is dead.
He writes his piece, only half lies, does Zeb,
Sick with the shame of it; worse
When it comes out, next day, in print
And makes him glad. So he makes good, shows them,
Becomes one of them: worse, and worst, accepted
In the group, the newest creeping lout.
It is ill, ill, as his flesh knows. Zeb, Zeb,
Save yourself. Contrive some end to it.
Get out.

Newcastle was more
Of the same, without the war.
Jesmond now, a small hotel:
Where a waitress, dark, lovely, large, Irish,
Filled Zeb with lust and love,
And he too slight, shy, young to be considered.
No war of which to write;
No bombs then, no dust.
A warm and cheering, busy place;
Zeb junior partner to Freddie Straw, photographer,
All energy, and tasteless mid-blue suits,
All nerves, rapid and slick, but a mentor-friend
Lavishing inventiveness on Zeb; he'd lend
Him aggression that, had he been on the receiving end,
Would have made Zeb sick.
The little two-man office stood
At the Gallowgate end of United's ground
Far from home and Boro, yet
To plant small loyalties to grow, years on, a football lark,
A ramble in St. James's Park.
Freddie buzzed cheerfully, not still
Ever; Zeb flourished on his zest, ideas tossed
In with his photographs. All was success,
Pap-print piled up. Flattery for Zeb,
Even post-war prospects from the very fount
Of creeping. Zeb, it is ill,
And so are you. Lost, lost,
Lost still.

The circle broke. He joined
The Air Force, having learned
A speck of the world. For,
In his farce-interview,
Some elderly, established voice
Asked (duly, as forecast): "Why do you wish
To join, lad?" And if
You could pronounce, without
A smile, with earnest, earnest flash of eye,
"I want to fight
In the air, Sir, to fight and fly,"
Then you were in, and earning,
So long as you did not laugh,
And he did not;
Which shows that Zeb was learning.

Then he was sent
To a stone fairyland. A university –
And I speak seriously –
In a castle. His mates were
Rather an intimidating lot,
All single, free, from public schools
Chiefly – and Zeb apart again.
He shared a room with Wat, from Bradfield
Coll., and Budleigh Salterton;
Nut brown, laconic quiet, superiority
Unspoken (Zeb's first contact with the Crust),
His uncle an Air Marshal;
Which did not prevent dear Wat, just learning laughter,
From being dead, remarkably soon after.

It was a place of hints
Never amounting, quite, to reality.
Confusing shafts of light, scenes

43

Live in themselves, never a whole.
The big, weak-lovely lad who, they said,
Could run fast, beyond the imagining;
But Zeb, confused, not known, being built for speed,
Caught him without much trouble on the rugby field.
Half the day we played at students, gowned;
At physics, mechanics, maths applied;
Zeb lost, but with right partner at his side
Experiments worked out, just as they should.
Mysterious things, diagrams and formulae,
Could easily be learned by heart, as poetry;
So it emerged somehow, that winter,
That Zeb became – laughter forbidden – B.Sc. (Inter).

In afternoons we played
At being in the Raf, at law,
Navigation, drill, and boring things
Like lectures on the upper atmosphere,
Wasted on us, having no wings.
Teas at the café by the Wear,
Dances with girls from colleges, and beer;
All this a carousel, with Zeb confused, apart.
Yet loving this and that, and all compressed
In the night he, all energy and full of beer,
Late, climbing the keep to slide illegally in,
Falls off his ledge, on rope of helpful mountaineer,
Swings out, over a city of sleep;
Tails billowing, formally dressed for flight,
Out, out under stars, over the river,
Startling a thousand monuments (all
Medieval, having seen all; gargoyles
Now thought asleep, delivered from evil)
As some great dancing, arching bat,
Some flapping joy-delirious kicking devil.

Odd, years on, that oft-repeated grind
Of every day be lost, left somewhere behind.
Thus Zeb's reception by the R.A.F.
(Reception was their word; they called the place
Aircrew Reception Centre). How was he received?
The marching, bullshit and all that
Must have filled the weeks;
All of that gone, but still present, ever
Is Corporal Stuckey: tall, features suffused with red,
Jug-eared; face in near-permanent snarl,
Resenting; thick unmixed bile,
Hatred on tap, fresh by the minute.
You would not call him unintelligent;
He had that quick irascible awareness,
Almost a prescience, which now would understand
That arson is lately quite all right
Between consenting adults.
He copulated verbally his way
Ever so carefully, with the Word
Placed, not normally before each other word,
But before the syllable. "Fucking-U-fucking
Niv-fucking-versity fucking-Air-fucking Squad-
Fucking-ron: I'll fucking-show fucking-you."
Or: "Fucking Zeb-fucking-u-fucking-lon
Fucking Mac-fucking-Swine, fucking come
Fucking up fucking here and fucking get the
Fucking mail. Fucking none for fucking you,
Fucking Mac-fucking-Swine." (I do apologise
For this flood of profanity. I am
Embarrassed. Zeb now sits in his garden, giving not a
     damn
What people think. But I, as you must know, am at liberty
Not to report, on those occasions – few but strong – when
     he

45

Sinks to the language of the lavatory;
Although I do, for accuracy's sake, this once;
And you (and I) can skip over, and not look.
Come on, Zeb, let's get on with the book.)
He (not Zeb, but Corporal Stuckey) ran us round
In wire-wool uniforms, that hottest day, Lord's Cricket
   Ground,
Until you stepped across the bodies; the usual
Venom in the voice, turning to ecstasy.
Zeb heard, they'd later dropped
Three sandbags for his head, from the fifth floor
Of the high flats we slept in, but they missed;
Showing, as yet, deficiency
In bombing theory. He survived;
For Zeb, years later in the war,
In his home town, passed Stuckey in the street;
Still bilious, still a corporal, still roseate,
And failing to salute. Zeb
Struggled a bit, then let it go;
Unsure yet whether he was playing
Pseudo-Christ, or just a fool. But seen
Perspectively, as they do say,
Stuckey was no more than
Memorable extreme, the creature of a day.
We met his contrary, hours later
In Brighton: dear ginger little witty Corporal
Banter, who marched us up the populated streets,
All bark and brimstone; and who,
Once round the corner, laughed
His Halt, said Bugger Off, quietly;
And left us to enjoy
Our days beside the sea.

46

Not much connection between outside and in
On Zeb's solo: the little Tiger Moth
Chugged along at twelve hundred feet
Neatly enough, circuiting Sywell airfield.
All as it ought to be: fine day,
Green grass down there; even the dread empty seat
Seemed natural. But inside, the heart
Pumped, echoed; fingers, responding to approved
    mnemonics,
Felt dimensions away, not his.

All went along its rails
When, landing, the grass blades focussing
Nicely, heart now leaping into throat,
And hard to swallow back,
Chance struck. This time, benign:
For we, the plane and Zeb as one,
Were taxiing in triumph, he amazed,
Awestruck; he had felt
No wheels touch. If you have once
Been gifted with perfection, you will know.
In all his later, dull customer life
On endless airlines, worn commercially
Down to secure correctness, *that* was to be
Only once again.

Wanting to fill his second seat once more,
That evening, summer, the joy welling
From the guts, he found a gurdy-fair
In Northampton, and a girl there
Young, compact, interested. He followed her, an age,
Too full of himself, his own joy, to stir
Shyness. She waited, spoke,
Made her warmth plain. Then,

47

Then nothing; she went into her house, shut
The door; he, back through the town, and to
His Nissen hut.

Exultation
Is solitary: devours, never brooks rival;
Does not share.
And solo has more meanings
Than one.

Convoy, from Liverpool, with
The *Thomas H. Barrie*: who?
Zeb never ascertained, but American,
Surely, like the ship.
It had carried black troops
On its last voyage, they said:
No time to clear, to set in order
Before this sailing.

           You were quartered
Four decks down: a sweetish
Faintly rotting, sweat-warm smell,
Just perfumed on its surface by
Hot engine oil. Five-tier bunks;
Thirty wondering, unsure Raf half-sleepers
Per cabin. Seas rough to heavy, torturing.
Winter fighting into Spring, the *Thomas*
Zig-zagged its way across the days
And nights, with all the rest.
Meals far more of a test
Than U-boats: you lined up
On even lower deck, well below water;
All engine thud, oil and brass;
Rhythmic din deafening, and
Stood, an hour; guts murmur warnings;
A sad snake-line of apprehension
All the ship's length,
Emerging dizzy at the end
Into the white, brilliant-lit mess hall, to eat.
This voyage had two kinds of light:
Out, gloom-grey of the sea;
In, fluorescent; walls, bread shocking white.
You stood to eat, at trestle tables
High – why all at neck-height?

Swaying, everything together, emetic ghosts:
Bread white, whiter than snow; sweet, with
Piles of sweet pickles; sweeter rich butter, recalled
Dimly in cinema-memory;
Rocking shock to guts adjusted,
Half, to engine oil, and pre-
Shrunk by war-dark bread at home.
In the ten days (and he kept
Trying), Zeb managed
No food at all, except
One small dry orange. He slept
By choice, in fresh, O freshest, air
On the open top-deck boards, all
Spray and roar and angles there,
To roll bodies around, and cold.

On day nine we stood
Off Newfoundland, watching two
Convoy ships burn, soon
To sink: it seemed to take
Hours; Zeb wishing he were over there
Sinking too; then primly glad, not;
Then undecided. Next, a glimpse
Of New York, as we took
A train, north.

The Maritime Provinces
Are stark and bare;
The houses wooden, old:
Weather fierce, cold.
The battering has been
By the years;
Places lost in space,
A remnant torn
Off some foothold
Hopeful once;
Wearing out,
Near worn.

In the drugstore,
Oasis.
Sodas, chrome, lights, milk
Limitless, indulgence, wealth.
Zeb drank about
Eight pints of milk and cream
His first night out;
Which soon
Cut him in two
And made him sick;
Retched back his greed again,
Gobbeting, some Spenserian
Grotesque of excess,
Atoning.

Once, a war away, put aside,
They licensed me to do
All I wished
Above a prairie of my own;
A yellow, endless stretch
Below a blue bowl;
And all between,
My own, to ravish
As I wished.

I would make, force you, to see
How deeply gold the earth,
Yellow, the grain in sun;
How falsely blue that sky.
How lit the invisible air between,
Chill on the cheek;
How it would touch, make you gasp, cry
To have to place it back, and say
In Canada,
A war away.

I fly, unsinged, unharmed,
A moth about the sun,
Yet roar
As well as any other
Meteor.
If earth can move, and be
About the sun
Why so can I, and I can move
The sun,
For me.

Climb, climb high, higher
Up the blue, assuming that you shall climb through.

Before you do, pull back the stick.
Cease, hold on; all colours mix
In swirl; hang, hang on the straps,
Feel the blood rush: the longest moment lived
Yet. Then, still hold back, do nothing; but
Keep rudder straight. Sweep down,
Put your heart back; finding the rails
The tracks in air, to the familiar,
The world again in place, and I
Did put it there.

Joy is two-dimensional:
Inside to out.
This, this has three:
A trinity.

I can reverse
The universe;
Can turn the world
Upside down: replace
Endless gold grain,
Turning it blue,
And rock it back again
With a small, yellow
Biplane.

Zeb can re-live, at will
The freezing, frozen struggle
Home from school, when he was four;
His definition, (owned through years)
Of wretchedness, extreme: known now only
At a remove, and bringing back
A child-grown-stranger, with his tears.

It was time to meet another cold:
Loose word, cold, covering a thing
Unrelated, unmet; ambushing.
Wind, blowing across endlessness
In all directions, given form by
Snow loosed from frozen iron, blowing to mist.
It could have been Siberia
In emptiness: the way wind cut
Through clothes, head, body, making you grab-gulp
The air in, hating its pain.

He sat and stood two hours
Warming up an Anson;
Both engines blazing, throttles
Open full: each temperature needle
Thrust firm against its little
Post of minimum, nothing less dreamed of.
Temperature outside, minus sixty-eight;
And in the wind, something lower, not within mind-
     gauge,
Either, for imagining.

                    Excused in the end,
Engines defeated, he was free
To go back to the curved hut, hear
Wind scream, battering the dark;

54

Curse, argue, fight; hate the others
Entrapped.

It was called Estevan:
Snow fields, space, one grain elevator.
He longed for towns remembered; even the last,
Moose Jaw, seeming a city now;
Where you could hurry
Doorway to doorway, using each
To unfreeze the nose, breathe painless breath
And reach, in the end, a drugstore,
Diner-heaven, hot, with girls and
Cooking fat.

Time for background – such as they often print
In italics. *Canada.*
You reached a place in it
Via blurred unending trees, space again,
By train: dusty, hot, double-
Windowed; seats a dust-rust-brown,
Penetrating sore, spike-velvet.

       A settlement: lake,
Hill, huts, runways; there you too were
Planted, as for ever. There
You drank, over-drank:
(Faint memory of tumbles, errant wives, bored
On lawn, in front of mess);
Flying, over trees, more space
To other lakes; navigation flights, where
You could follow rail lines, read names
On tiny stations. Bombing patterns,
Close grouped or wide, good/bad; neither
Seemed to matter – the future hinted? Ditto
Bullet scores on drogues. Boredom.

O Zeb, could I have reached you then
With what I know now, you'd have been conned
Less easily into the mould; have been given
Something beyond the brevet on your chest
For chasing girls. Was there, then, nothing in your brain,
To understand? Why, you were sold. It was
You who enskilled procured ones, you, purveyor
Of young herds for the Harris slaughterhouse.
Do not try now to justify, excuse
Your petty part in it, I know you knew
Only a little; never once made
One thought your own, persuaded into

The killing trade, where deaths could
Generate a thousandfold.
Know now, your debt – to have refused the blood-
   charade;
Stayed innocent. Nor would the blameshame, ugliness,
Have lasted longer than regret, standard regret
For those you trained to walk
Thoughtless as you, hapless into the dark.
Nine days' wonder, that regret, for nine day lives;
At a rough guess, say,
About three weeks.

Boredom.
Sunset-summer walks, winter shelter, warm
In room, in mess. Parties, leaves.
Zeb a badminton champion. Weekend passes;
Toronto, grey then: seven Sundays in a week;
Dry, but for beer parlours, tiled
Urinals where you poured it in
Rather than out, with the hoboes.
You could cheer the Maple Leafs, see
Shops all glitter-rich;
And go on leaves.

                 Like that
With Johnnie to Detroit, he being there
Engaged. But what with bars, staggering
Hospitality; girls in shops who gave
Us nylons (rare even there), and recovery,
He never reached fiancée until
Two hours before the train back. At
The station Zeb was duly, coldly greeted by the girl;
His friend disengaged. The train at last
Moved out: Zeb has met a girl
Named Blatherwick, full, promise-inflated. Between the
   coaches

Johnnie, heroic, sacrificing, pretends to fall asleep
Standing, while Zeb explores
Her incredibles. Then back
To boredom.

What did it come to
In the end? A going through motions
Considered necessary, but little to do
With what was waiting. Motions to turn out
The endless belt of unknowing, sacrificial flesh
And blood for the Butcher's bloody apron, fresh.
To think, the mindless movements Zeb performed
Helped turn them out; and now
After half-century's fond consideration, rumination,
And so many dead, they contribute
Towards a butcher's statue.

Zeb stepped off the Island ferry.
The mature lady, with her shopping,
Asked him to tea, as friend
Might, back at home:
Starting a mystery
That would educate, slowly, in the end.

She was English, Sussex:
Canadian a quarter-century, planted.
She had the simple power
Beliefs give, with authority
From an old beauty, living on.
Personality ruled, overwhelmed. Husband
Just there, gentle, withdrawn; a nice man;
To an extent incidental, a little dead.

               The house
Full of uniforms: five, six, always
Back at home again; eating, talking,
Going into the city, lounging
In sun, imbibing kindnesses
From a stream; Zeb, somehow
At the centre of it. Freely given,
Given, his birthday dinner
At the hotel, *King Edward*; parcels
To Zeb's family, and for long
After the war. Things.

The giving slightly recognised: a plaque
From the Queen, always "Her Majesty"
(Zeb, hypocrite, keeping his terms dark).
The mystery stayed: goodness, poured out
But not inhuman, not unmixed. The Christian Science
Pushed a bit strong and, years after,

Was opened, read with shock, Zeb's fruity bed-letter
Never allowed to reach him. You forgive:
Nothing's unmixed, but still, goodness
Not broken there.

His last sight of her, ill,
Was of her playing the piano for him, still,
In her nineties years.
He did learn, in the end,
What the power had been, behind
His half-century of receiving, and before:
Called goodness, which barely
Clarifies – it should be written, being no more
Than the unconditional wishing
Of well, of well,
Reasonless, to someone
Other, and strange.

A girls' choir came to sing.
Allow, of course, for the days, the flatness
Of routine; the sudden new silk dresses, lights
All glittering for the eyes,
Music; all heighten, deceive, idealise.
But there was one, slight, lit
On the front row; Zeb's eye rests
On the image; in one instant-change
All else ceases. Be reasonable.
What Zeb took in is now a list: black hair, long, parted;
White skin; eyes grey, level, showing
Rightness behind. You cannot list an aura,
A power round her, and an armour
In the air, implying, stating,
This is the thing, the thing itself, heard of
When the book-myths teach
Of beauty. Keep your distance; you may reach
Only the awe you feel, no more.
Others, surer than Zeb, felt that; stayed far.
Yet, paradox, Zeb, gaping shy,
Should overleap all that: they did speak
And were fond. Meetings, surprised,
Exulting; all harmony, aphysical,
Never quite believed, then, or after.
Fired, feared for future, unknown,
Impossible; war, continents apart.

Zeb stands in the snow, in a park,
With this girl in a red coat.
They hold, each the other. Remember, remember.
He leaves, knowing this is such
Where impossibility presents its bill, much
And more. Tempted, he does not write. Years fade.
They do meet, and are friends.

61

Is, then, love a given energy, surplus,
Indestructible, that merely changes form,
According to physics' law
Losing no force, having no ends?

Two of us on leave, one older-wiser:
There was, admittedly, a war on, but
They took *The Chief* to California.
Chicago was hospitality; a bar;
A warm crowd put them on the train.
Kansas City was a waitress
Most ill-disposed, when ham
Could not be ordered in the way
She wanted it pronounced.
The Canyon. A few steps forward,
The breath stops. You can never see
Possessively: observe, try to fix; then
Light makes a panorama, quite
Different, fleeting, again, again
Until you surrender.

San Bernardino: orange
May blossom in the air, and everywhere.
We had hosts – more Toronto giving –
Who took us in. *Earl Carroll's*: a snipe-
Comedian called Pinky Lee attacked our Limeyness;
A starlet, one June Lang, warm, opposite.
There was a dinner at a country club,
Our host's, which turned into a party.
Zeb, head full of films, and twenty
Years achieved alive,
Lined up twelve double
Rum and orange, and drank all down.
He – it now has to be he-another, since
Consciousness ceased – said Goodnight, apparently,
Nicely, to all, was driven back
A hundred miles, befouling the car's side;
Was put to bed by his hostess;
Dreamed of soaring, effortless;

63

Slides through space, towards the moon;
Closer, closer, till he thought
To smash his head against the great pale ring,
Which jolted him awake, focussing, becoming
The circle of a chamber-pot, a thing
Placed there, for his convenience.
And it was morning.

Nothing could wait. On the trail, early back,
Wonder on wonder, breathlessly. Brown Derby,
Hollywood, Santa Anita track:
To see it all, Zeb must turn from the knees,
So he can move his eyes.

Hostess came later;
Two thousand miles, to meet;
Tucked into his uniform pocket
Two hundred dollars
Three separate times, and said,
"I know you boys don't have
Much money."
O, Zeb! Zeb!

Air gunner, from Newfoundland:
A slightly madder version
Of Douglas Fairbanks (Junior) and
With same small moustache, high forehead;
And far, far round the bend, they said –
A condition acquired from somewhere
In the Far East. "By the living God,
MacSwine," each statement would start out,
Voice mixed with roaring laugh, to penetrate
Each cleft and corner, everywhere,
Like vacuum opening up to air.

Zeb was supposed to check
His lectures to young aircrew, those on gunnery
(I know my Byron: there'll be no rhymes like *nunnery*);
No need to visit, or to move at all;
Phrases would float down corridor, and bounce
Off wall: "Remember, by the living God,
You're British boys. You may not go,
Dunking your love-muscle
Just anywhere .... In formation, know,
Among the flak and searchlight rays:
Port aircraft must corkscrew to port,
Starboard, to starboard; but the centre
One undulates for several days ..."

Zeb saw him last after the war,
In the huge lounge at the Strand
Palace, behind blinding Argyle socks and
Feet upon the table: voice welcoming
Zeb by the living God, laughter
Freezing a hundred conversations.
He married a quiet, retiring girl, of course.
The last words from him came through

Zeb's Canadian "mother"; he scarcely
Knew her, but wrote from Newfoundland:
"Tears stain the paper as I write,"
He said in pain, as his home became
A new Canadian province.
It's a bit unlikely, then,
They'll be making more like him
Again.

Why should two airmen, randy
In drink, make dates
Within two hours, with
Seven pairs of girls,
Possible love-mates;
Watch them assemble,
A little crowd,
Surveying each other
Doubtfully;
Watch, from pub opposite,
Keeping away?
Stay with the loaded
Unwarlike table,
Salads and rabbits
Available all day.

Zeb will admit
The shame, and risks,
If you will not
Give this
To psychiatrists.

At Ludford Magna, the airfield, huge,
Had the village in its middle,
Between runways. The Nissen huts
Were rough, chill. Bicycles teetered in ruts.
Buses few; it was ten miles
To Louth, and ten
To Market Rasen.

Great Ludford!
Zeb looked for Ludford
Parva, small;
And, being trained in navigation,
Failed to find that at all.
Forty years on
He sought Ludford
Magna again.
Leaving just cornfields,
That, too, had gone.

Lindholme was different,
Brick-Georgian permanent,
Comfortable.
What remains there?
A race won; sunset
Evenings; the Green Tree pub.
Walks with the blessed, lovely Waaf girl,
Gold-blonde, substantial
(Zeb lost again);
Back by the runways
Into our ditch, encompassing, then
Blotting out station, Raf,
War, world;
Again, again.

The station is still there;
It had prisoners, then.
A U-boat man, taken early on,
Regarded a bending Waaf's rear end
With so hopeless a longing, that
Zeb was touched; became his friend.
He carved a ship; gave it to Zeb.
They left; the place, then
A relic of the war.
It has new prisoners now,
But Englishmen.

An odd figure, Zeb, as if
Just created for his time: half-war, half-peace.
Young enough (twenty three) still,
But with deliberation; movements
Older: cover, for ignorance
Of where he is, what for, where
He's been, where going.
A new uniform – cord trousers, old
Sports jacket (what can you do
With a blue chalk-stripe
Demob suit?); he rides
A new green bike with gears,
New-invented storage batteries
For lights: they don't recharge, though rechargeable.
The whole a grand gratuity-gesture
Of twenty pounds, and not affordable.

There he goes, one of the lucky ones,
Survived, pedalling; brand-new, old
Student. He lives
In Lumley Castle, in a cubicle
Eight feet by six, but private
If you ignore the space
From floor to plywood walls, and that
From walls to ceiling.
His main confusion is, he does not know
What he might, possibly, be capable of knowing, so
Begins a pass degree: French, English,
Economics (and some rowing).

The green bike moves, as of itself,
The miles to Durham; so lost is he,

Preoccupied, though just aware
Of mining villages gliding by,
One called Pity Me.

The city is small. Old beauty
Piled on its near-island,
High, obvious. Yet, behind,
A threat, a doubt, a Northernness.
Not like Oxbridge worn beauty
That whispers, "I take you in; join my tradition:
You will prosper." No: this snarls a little, cries, "You
Are alone here: world is doubt.
Future, like history, is storm."
The gargoyles are alive. Loveliness is
There, but hard. Old carved stone seems
Near to reach out, to scour the skin,
Sensing the unsure.

         Zeb did not know
Of the Scots' slashing in the cathedral
(Never entering there, in his learning years!)
But it was in tune. The current ones
In charge, unsure themselves, like chameleons
On the old walls, coloured by mild menace
Not understood. Routine of days was refuge.
Zeb, in a tight group of five
Looked for, and found his laughter;
Missed breakfast, and most lunch.
The Great Hall of Durham Castle,
Overseen by grave divines
Does not accord with sausages, gravy,
Grey potatoes. Mornings had
The odd lecture, astutely chosen
(See piece, close by, on those);
The afternoon was sport: rugby,
Hockey, running; sculling best;
The rota high tea in a reluctant
Host's room, with ungrateful culinary

Critiques. Evenings: cinemas, fish and chips, beer.
Work scarcely entered in. You needed
To write some essays: Zeb learned (reading a little)
That if he piled a few bricks of opinion
Mortared by logic, buttressed with quotes,
His fast-built edifice could be well received.
It was embezzlement, but there was nonetheless
Some growth in knowing, feeling, to it all; most
From friends, routine. Memory chooses
The special, beyond logic, habit: those, it loses.

Zeb must have, earlier, cycled, bus'd his way
Through cruellest winter, ice and mountain
Snow; recalling, now, no flake of it.
But he still knows, one bucket
Of daily coal can heat no room
In an unheated castle.
He hears the bedders, cheerful,
Grotesquely underpaid, speak
Geordie greetings it took terms
To understand. Come back again,
Again, those sausages, bland at best,
Or burnt, a choice, with
Grey mash, and dark mystery lumps.

There were ex-Majors, needing
To be in by ten; two who
Pretended to sign in, escaped and ran
Within, causing communal punishment.
Then a strike, students camping out
On Palace Green: only an hour
Before Authority gave in. Hint
Of a distant future! Zeb, persuaded,
Bought a share in one Harold Reuben, greyhound,
Who never won, because he never ran.
Bathrooms were distant: see, see

Again, the pitcher of night-pee-freeze
Cast from high window of the keep,
Arch, pale gold, into the bare back at dawn
(Just the bathing trunks on, fawn,
As he touched toes)
Of the Master, Gen. B.B. McCrap and Sneeze.

There was a life of its times.
The Prof., he who chose the little
Honours group; let Zeb in; expelled half,
Boomed condescendingly two years
At the dozen survivors. Large, large;
Blimp-like, but stately; red face,
The white, flat hair, white
Moustache, eyes pale, waterish;
Voice deep, from the chest.
A sort of Butcher Harris magnified,
Without blood-lust. He wrote poems:
Slim volumes, all bulls and balls and maleness,
All rural power and swelling;
Himself well within the closet; standard
Forties practice. A member of
The Athenaeum.

          There were favourites
Young, fresh-faced, but nothing
Really untoward. Just an aura
Not proven, not significant; all within bounds,
And justice surviving in results. His lectures
Boomed majestic generalities: Clare
"May well have had Something to Say –" Comments
On essays: "Mmmmm" (boomed) – "Something
May Come Through." Not much use
To us.

He had, with some luck, discovered famous
Journals; leading him to Yale
Where, five years on, was Zeb,
Who saw, then, beneath the veil,
The magisterial mask. He was unsure, awed
At being part of Boswell, high in the industry;

Becoming playful-human, though, to
Zeb's pretty, unsuitable wife. But still
Defensive, angry, resenting the literary
Power-fame-cash-establishment
Having his papers.

Kind,
Embarrassed to be caught kind;
Scared, lost, having an operation abroad, adrift,
Far from his own walled garden.
We looked after him a little,
Not long before he died.

No one considers lectures.
They're simply there, and may be
Anything, from fascination
To cold air.

In time, you get a scale, like
A little xylophone;
Five notes on ours.
Try to be fair, according looks
Chronologically, by field, just like
The lit. crit. books.

Herbie, well-known, half famous
Antiquarian, and antique, near dodder;
Steeped deep in Durham. Dusty, not
Unpleasant; remote song, from remoter age.
Our translations fodder,
Mere stimulus, for rambling
Anglo-tangent Saxon-tangent
Which spread out, out
As circles in a pool,
From unexpected
To unconnected;
(The odd bright drop
Small, small),
Reminding you
Of what you somehow knew.
Really no fool;
Harmless to all.

Then, Beech. O he was good, known
Even in the town to be. Sleek,
Efficient. Shakespeare's portrait
Well fleshed out. All was

Ordered, logic-full; you knew
Where you were, had been, were set
To go: "Last time we met,
We ...." Better yet,
Alive, most alive, convincing;
All sprang to greater life when he
Would quote: actor, and good;
With the voice, and brains. You could
Not help but learn, beneath
The polish and performance. It may have
Been, a bit too pat, too smooth,
Well-oiled; certainly a bit too
Scientific; able to kill
A little, with over-calculation.
But that is to cavil.

We now approach the Age
Of Reason. Dear, old-seeming, hiding, hidden one,
Maligned, correct, frog-like, a little
More than shy, alone: J.B.,
He of the hesitant delivery.
What stick, lampoons, he took!
But if you should
Happen to listen – and few did –
The things he said, were good,
Sound, incisive, interesting; even
Provocative. Modest (of course)
And right – without that sense
Of something a bit awry, mistuned, beneath
The quality, as you got with Beech.
He was, moreover, kind, behind
The correctness, if you approached. Nearly
No one did.

Prof. boomed his generalities;
We tried to follow in the text;

Little to gain that way: we
Were glad when it was over, free
Then, from Authority. As he
Would say, little Came Through.
What did he want,
Intellectually, from you?

Last, the young one:
Fast, slick, and from Leeds;
Preaching the moderns (they,
According to the syllabus
Were unborn anyway).
Somehow he managed
By chaos in his talk
To pre-enact that
To come. A prescience
Wasted on us.

What can you learn from this?
Order is good, logic of steps;
Reminders; energy, acting by rote,
Persuasion. Say what you'll try,
And what comes next. Support by quote.
Read, bring to life; read as meaning;
Ideas, yes, but feelings too; interpret as you know.
Ask questions (*they* rarely did);
Wait (they less at ease than you) until they answer.
Don't let go, until you've forced
At least a bit of actual thought;
And do not hide delight
When (sometimes with wit)
They penetrate a bit
Deeper than you.

Aim
(No avoiding this) at the few committed

(With greatest luck, about a third).
Others, the More beloved by politicians,
Needing to be elsewhere,
Can come – some will – to talk
As individuals, of their despair.
Help as you can; explain
Judgements – on essays especially;
Support what you've judged, and make it plain.
Note if they come again;
For some, a very few lost ones, despite all
Atrocities performed on them in schools
Can grow interested. Most
Injured too much, meagrely equipped,
Stay fools.

Escaping pain, and guiltily,
Zeb, with raffish, half-degenerate Hal,
Half-friend, went to Italy;
And with Hal's promise of return
In emergency;
On motor-bike – pillion – all a race
New to Zeb, with rucksack huge
Driving his arse ever
Deep, into sore furnace.

They danced a Bastille Day
In Paris, in the streets,
With two girls, friendly; both put off
By Hal's urgent, bumptious
Assumptions. France flashed by, then
Alps; that evening they descend
Into a sepia air; (say
What you may, it was, it was a sepia air
And sepia land) to Turin, which proved an end.
Destination had been the Lakes, but
They got no further, magic-held.
Shops in colonnades, cheap in strange luxuries
(And Italy late occupied?)
Zeb has still a flagon, silver,
The green liqueur that the sun shines through,
Forty years on. The cheap, lovely hotel,
Opposite the palace called Madama:
First people-charms;
First dinner on a balcony
Over the square; first real spaghetti,
First wonder, at the new deliciousness;
First young and friendly arms
Of girls, professional, living in hotel.
Hal easily fell, Zeb resisting-scared.

81

He had to play the man, when
Later, he won the toss
(Cash enough only for one) in the first-
Class, ten-shilling house, and was given then
A joy, a beauty unsuspected and
Not often equalled since.
Everything was friendliness,
All Welcome, everywhere:
The neat, charm-elderly
Bosco, sophisticated, showed
Them round. You could rent
A clean large room
For half-a-crown a week;
Eat from the market, live sublime
On nothing; learn the tongue;
Devour the fun, be young;
Except there was no time.

Zeb knew he had to go.
The promise broken, he stood,
By train, the length of France;
Was back in time, for
His father's agonies to come.
He has been back, half-seeking
The magic, but the sepia air
Was changed, garish, all colours now, a maze
Bright, unyielding, time altering place
To something other, busy, uniform
With the rest of days.

Light behind his eyes, charm on the lips,
Loving of women; our Mother followed him,
One business trip; saw him with one, or more
Of *Them*, and always remembered, always.
He was warm to me, with something more
Than warmth, behind the eyes.

Touchy, reasonless like a child, with angry fits.
I did the fires, wiped the hearth, got the coal in;
Made firelighters of piles, piles of newspapers;
All routine; the same, and harder, for my sister.
Then, the sudden Saturday drives, all re-scrubbed, re-
   cleaned
Till the rage was calmed, played out. Then,
For no reason – "Where're *you* going? – Well,
You're *Not*." You stayed quiet, waiting;
And like a child he'd come to be forgiven;
Mutter something fond, and you went.
I was the father to the man.

He bullied me, and he bullied
My dog; and my dog
Loved him, more than he loved me.
I was puzzled, then.
What do you make of that?

I see the Firm's big car (rare in the thirties);
The samples constantly repacked;
Love-colours, dimly sexual, smooth;
Repacking uselessly helped by me.
I see his dinners the days that he was home,
The adult glamour of chop, chips and beans.
But in the evening, after my tea,
The smell of the near-empty plate

And the chop bone, given to me.

I stood each Saturday
At the main road corner,
Pressed against the railings,
Watching the traffic; read
The Cricket Festival poster
Next to me (*Gentlemen v. Players?*)
Twenty times, knowing each name,
Waiting, waiting the hours,
Watching the clock in the school tower
Not move; so the White Horse pub
Never closed – not to me. But it did
To him; so he came in the end, and all
Was worthwhile. Did I say
I loved him?

The War when, Air Raid Warden,
He could do nothing
At his age, ruptured from the last one:
Artillery, heaving shells.
And after all the years I saw
Him pressing at his side,
Queer, it seemed to me, that he,
A corporal, de-striped for drink,
Should, in my time, not admire
The King's commission, uniform, and wing
On the chest. Nor did I know, not then,
It was because he saw the entire fraud,
Each trick of the embezzlement, the show
That dragged in the young, like romantic
Drunken beery ones after the rugby game.
It was because he knew
What I know now.

The parting was by cancer of the bowel.
He half-believed the spurious hope they gave
For operations, one and two;
His comment just the tiny moans of pain.
I ran away, because I could not bear
The sweet cloy-smell of nature when reversed;
Not, at least, from him.
But I returned, and, somehow to reach, communicate,
Played the record, of Hamlet when alone.
The beauty attained him; the unknown touched.
He died, in courage, hopelessly beyond my reach.
His face was still:
The forehead I touched, cold.
And in this brain,
This hand, that moves and writes,
He is there.

Confined by now herself to bed,
His mother was upset, disturbed, with
Feelings she could not word; fears
From his father's ashes in their box.
They had to go, the night they had arrived.

Setting was right enough. Wind
Howled, buffeted; rain
Fell as streams or sheets, selected
Random, by wind. No dark:
Black. Zeb, armoured
In Wellingtons, oilskins,
Sou'wester, cycle clips,
Strapped, well-wrapped, the Box
To the back of his old bike,
Tall, gearless, a relic stolen from
The Raf; set off at six.
Blown off, and Wellingtons
Nicely full after ten yards,
He progressed: wetness no ill
After saturation point; wind and black
Difficult. In the three flat miles, it
Helped to be torn at
By the actual, outside,
Relieving memory within.
Then the country two-mile hill, walked up
To the moors, exposed to all, on top of all.
Nothing solid there: half-seeming
Silhouettes; some hint of road.
He felt the wind, knew the dark;
Then did see clear, illumined,
The sunny Sundays at this loved, loved place.
Afternoons; his father, pipe in mouth,

Bowling underhand; felt the bat in
His hand: Mother already less than mobile (a bit
Like Zeb now) sits on the rug, among
The picnic things; the old car, upright, tall.
Chum, the dog, has chased a rabbit
Into the stone wall.
All this, across years, in the dark.

                  He knelt;
Scattered the ashes, in all ways
With all his strength, into the wind,
But most toward the cricket pitch.
Rode back, downhill now, altered.
Something fitting in the loss of it, some birth
Of gain. Arrived, at midnight,
There was, sudden, the gift:
A kind of bargain, six hours, then a new
Day; new quiet. A thing done
Bringing an order, something right;
New-glad, that can not
Be discussed.

In summer student days
Of reading lists, unread,
Zeb worked: seller of tickets, taker
Of cash for sundaes, drinks, and ice cream cones;
Meeting the British holidaymaker,
Forging some links: odd ones
Would even ask him for a date,
And not *vice versa*; which might suggest
That possibilities were good. Not so
In the event: no vice at all; every chaste mate
Resisting touch, embrace of chest,
As well as other and profounder sorties.
If you should manifest some doubt of this, it was
The Nineteen forties.

It would be reasonable to envisage
Some better prospects from the staff, all rough
Young girls from Durham mining village.
Zeb was the only male: you'd guess
He'd be electric, keen and dirty.
Again, not so; when chance came, he would fail;
The girls tough, strong, and shirty;
Besides being sternly managed by
Miss Edgebottom, far tougher still.
Large, large in breast and bum;
Chins, hair upswept, a small pink ribbon on.
A daughter of the West (Riding of Yorks.), she'd
Line up her girls like soldiers on parade,
Or chorus in some music-farces;
And Zeb, arriving late, would hear
Her peroration, "... you'll do just what I said,
While you've holes in your arses."

She had a good, warm, well-protected heart, and rude.
There was a warmth about it all;
A special, little, special interlude
Seen exemplary when Zeb would call
At evening parade, interrupting some
Harangue. "I've cashed up, Miss Edgebottom."
Sternness would melt to smile,
All motherly: "Aye, bugger off Luv, go 'ome."

NINETEEN FIFTIES

She had that aquiline, bustled beauty
From hazy *Floradora* years, before
Wars became Great. The beauty changed, adjusted,
Never died. A simple lady, simple life, all
Family, always money-pressed. She
Believed in rules, being shocked
By husband, saying she could not forgive
But did, if not forget. Zeb shocked her too,
Yet she seemed, more easily, to put his crimes
Aside.

                 Her latter third of life
Confined to bed, immovable; the bed downstairs
In the small front room of the semi, neighbours
Ever dropping in. She cried, in the small hours
With the pain, rising some nights to screams;
Zeb, when he was there, out of his depth, appalled:
No moves to help left, nothing still possible;
Nothing to try. When it was less, of itself,
She could enjoy some days, cheerful, accepting;
Even remembering how
To laugh.

After the longing for relief, in the late days,
Her ambitions were as always: peace,
Routine; she had few desires, was
Not curious of anything beyond set range
Of home: abroad was never seen
Except as near-wicked. A life narrow,
Old-fashioned; but she had faith, knew
What she believed. Right was
Right, so solid you could touch it.

Once, she'd raised herself in bed, looked at Zeb,

93

Who took her photograph. He muses
On the face now, tries to connect the image
With his life: the grave to be tended,
Made different from the two foot-narrow strip,
The boyhood garden, dry hard earth
Along the back yard, pointless, undug, where no sun
    touched
And nothing grew; no single weed. Now
Years, as wedge, disconnecting, set between.
Nothing there, in the face, but simple love
Unqualified, only itself.
Nothing to say, when you see that
Once in one lifetime;
All else irrelevant.

So much is given, earned, owed,
That cannot be repaid.
Part of his sister was enough like Zeb:
Longing for life, love, family
(In her case), the physicality of things;
Like enough to make him know
The differences. Much, near all, given up
By her, to keep their mother's life
Going, possible; to make Zeb's life
As it was; her best years, given.
She bicycled to work, came home, cooked,
Nursed, kept a home.
Zeb, at his times there
From university, would make the tea,
Having some leisure touch for appetising
Food arrangement, would draw
Their mother's praise, comparing.
It was unfair, disturbing; putting
The moment beside the years.

Mother, sister: enough
To make Zeb, guilty, awed,
Into some sort
Of feminist;
Had that not since been changed
To an emetic.

There was a mixed, half-guilty leaving
For Zeb's new life: softened, hinting
At least for him, of hope, adventure,
Being young. Now – seeing his dead mother's printing
On tickets hanging still from trunks
Of forty years ago – it occurs to him
A little late: what was it for family, for them?
He had believed it would be for a year,
Or two, at most: went through
The partings; should then have caught
The train, but went first there
To say goodbye to her.

She was the face he'd seen
Across a bar; he then lost, fascinated;
She worldly, knowing. It had gone
Unevenly: rattling, callous at times, but the face
Still haunted. Now, the goodbye bed.

Uneven: she, sophisticate;
He starving, and naïf. Once
She'd wheeled him in, laid out
On trolley; sacrificial, bare like a chicken,
As a literal meal, for her. Then, she protesting
The newness of it, modesty and the rest;
First time for this and that; dish such as Beeton
Never thought of. Desire and anger racing
Each other, he'd refused, pettishly, to be eaten.
Why does he reject
What he's spent so long chasing?

             All of that
Put away, at this bed-parting: it led
Soon after, to the Letter: – bed-

Reminiscence, fruity; intercepted, opened by
His idealising mentor, and near-*Mater*
In Canada, causing some pain
(Webs, once woven, can stretch to odd extremes
Not undeserved), but that came later.
Now, having fulfilled some dream
A little hastily, he caught the train.

The station at St. Louis is a marvel
Of space; all Greek, echoes and marble.
Zeb stepped down from his giant train, overheated,
To be, a mere new student, warmly greeted
By his professor and department head,
Pleasant, slow-spoken, Southern, kind.
He drove Zeb round all the tree-lined
Avenues near the university;
Found him a room, rent-free
For baby-sitting for a family.
Zeb, esconced, was then invited to a party
(Table-tennis), professors senior, friendly, hearty.
Cheering, in new strange academe to pass
Warm, welcomed, easy, with no hint
Of establishment or class.

              Warmth was exceeded
By climate: temp. in the nineties;
Wet, moveless air. For Zeb's room
Nestling on roof, add thirty more degrees,
Even at night, even among the trees.
His natural greed suspended, he took in
One meal per day: lettuce and Spam, sliced thin;
Zeb never hungry (that quite new), desiring taste
Of nothing; soon twenty pounds the less, with tiny waist.

The family were O.K. Big Bill, a driving force
In Ford sales: football (U.S.) mad; ex-player though,
Who drank a bit; often not there. Wife, ginger, freckly,
Slight, fluttery, Southern, nice. Bill Junior, four or so,
The "baby," a bit of a small blaster,
But not so bad; and old in-law, Mrs. Pitts;
Nice again; a bit vague; most things passed her.

Zeb rode to work, on his green bike
Transported transatlantically; sight
New to natives, inciting laughter, frantic.
He rode on footpaths, rather like
Small runways, never used, so his
Alone; but when he tried
To walk on them, the police,
Full of suspicions, took him aside,
Forced him into their car
And ran him home, checking, and pained
To find that he went in, just where he'd claimed.

With no expenses, not so rich before, he
Could buy his mother a TV
Back in U.K.; which made her days, it was reported,
As well as later ones, more bearable, assorted.
The shops were huge, cheap, polished, full to groaning.
Were Zeb depressed (that rarely), he could buy
A summer suit, two-suiter travel case, new tie,
Instead of moaning.

He found friends, easy fellow
Students. *Waste Ball* in the office
Once friendly teaching done:
Ball thrown, nutcracker style
For points, at distant waste-bin;
Vastly wasteful of time.
A new-wed couple took Zeb in
As friend: evening at Beffa's bar, all leisure,
Wit, and beer; hamburgers, at two
Or four a.m., a pleasure,
Zeb never being one to haste day's end.

The work was simple; little to overcome
That had not been done before, at home.
There was the softball game, Eng. Dept.

Against snide Mathematicians,
Where Zeb, through luck, made winning
Hit; nearly caught up his teammate
On the bases, which would have been a shame,
Disaster, he then not knowing laws of game.
He had his luck; ran for a streetcar
Burlesque-bent, across a road:
Hit by a car, Zeb flew through the air
Some twenty feet, with no harm more
Than a small head-cut, and a side all sore:
Followed by a score, or more, of ambulance-
Chasing lawyers on the 'phone,
Who had to be resisted. Funny,
The driver turned out to be a student,
Just like Zeb, but with less money.

Burlesque, the Grand Theatre, down by the river;
Dear seamy streets, now cleared
(An Arch there now); but then
Zeb's spirit-home, his church.
The candy-butchers with their pitches;
The funny men, coarse, making time go
Between the strippers: Blaze Starr, Rose la Rose;
Orchestra blasting away, seductively.
One blonde, slim chorus girl with modest bust
Revealed each week on cue; a fascination,
Time-mark for Zeb; too wholesome far for lust.

The burlesque and the Browns
Were Zeb's twin peaks of love.
The hopeless baseball Browns,
Outshone perpetually by the fame of
St. Louis' serious team, the Cardinals.
The Browns! Although they won
One game in every five, by accident and chance,
Zeb, with few others, fell in love – romance.

He, knowing by then about baseball ballistics,
Would walk across the lovely campus grass
At dawn, before an early class,
And with his breakfast study Browns' statistics.
Though he once asked Browns' owner, personally,
Why Garver, great pitcher who could bat, should go
In number nine, there was no proper answer; and
Zeb still does not know.
At Browns games, in the near-deserted
Park, you could hear all the players said,
Free of crowd noise, and crowd; and learn
What not to do. They, the Browns,
Performed worse than their own farm
Teams, and had traditions
Such as an outfielder with but one arm.

As if directed by some fate, or charm, or cosmic law,
When Zeb's two years of heaven were removed,
He went to Harvard; the Browns, to Baltimore.
It had been two years of hospitality, made
Of warmth, free-given, and of youth delayed
In new and loving home, and loved.

Professor Bolinek was short, stubby, cheerful, Czech;
Large round head, flat silver hair; grin wicked; bull's look
About to charge: knowing more philology
Than could be dreamed of; yet not a full
Professor, since he lacked a book.
He would beseech Zeb out
To sundry bars for casual drink, or two
At most; but what Zeb did not know
At least at first, was this:
One drink, and, certain, two, brought metamorphosis:
No more respected academic oracle,
But drunken driver of a truck,
Staggering, swearing at top shout,
Propositioning everything in range,
If you did not intervene; and if you did
He was a massive handful, rare and strange.

At home, he had a wife, kind, motherly;
A budgerigar he loved, entitled Toby,
Fed cooingly by hand with beaksome particles;
Cage, luxury; soft-lined with scholars' articles.
Disdaining colleagues, he (Bolinek, not Toby)
Would come to watch the Wasteball; suggest the briefest
     drink,
And if you went, were lost night-long in every sink
That he could reach by taxi. Sometimes, for change,
He'd move up-market too: one night
Remembered vividly by Zeb, at the Starlight
Roof, Park Plaza Hotel: staid patrons
From spacious suburbs, chiefly matrons,
Mothers of students. Zeb hears yet
Bolinek, hitching short fat leg up on table
Taken by seven such, break wind
With epic roar, and slow deliberation,

Through night club, over roof to the surrounding night;
Will hear him, echoing to life's end, in full carouse,
"MacSwine, when 're we going to that whorehouse?"

He did complete his book, *Comenius;*
Became a full professor, voted in
As if he'd always been abstemious.
Pleasing, that; for he was much
Admired and loved, by students, Zeb and such;
Even a few professors.
But, shortly after, died.
Zeb, long gone, is unsure of diagnosis,
But would bet quite a lot it was cirrhosis.

The train arrived: he stepped out to cutting wind.
Everything closed; streets bare, except for snow;
Only the bars open, with the dancing girls;
Not hard to pass the day,
Evening, night.

          After all the routine ones
This girl was lovely: young, dark,
Pale; paler breasts, neither one seeming
To know whether to rise in dance
Or fall, settling for teetering
Just, just between. Zeb sat entranced.
After, she came to talk, wanting no drink;
Intelligent, simply nice; seemed,
Even, a bit intrigued; proposed
Meeting at five a.m., just
Up the street, when the club closed.

The street was empty, echoing, chill:
He knew to expect nothing; still
Deeper than that, some voice, defiant, seemed to say,
Then said, that she would come.
It was quite wrong: but to this day
He is convinced that what had been alive
Those minutes, was not such
That she had not meant to come,
And could not, for good reason.
That sort of fool he was, then;
Still is, and an aged one.

In the little city, Calumet,
The girls danced, much as usual
On the bars, but in the dark
Brandishing flashlights, directed
Precisely where you possibly suspected.
And while your keen attention at the bar
Is focussed frontwards on one star,
There is a drinking, a communion, and
A laying on of hands
By another; while Zeb's interest grew
And grew, yet a third hand he never thought to find,
Was in fact there, at hip pocket, behind.
He felt nothing; anyway, not that.

Outside, his money gone; snow wet,
Night black, cold: but they'd been kind
Enough to slip the billfold back: let
Into an inside pocket, previously,
Was still enough to ride back, easily
To Chicago. He had been just
Slightly clever, pre-stupidity.
The lesson is, when you're in cock
Of the walk mood, do put at least some cash
Inside your sock.

He got a little fellowship, that
First summer: took the train
To New Orleans, the office of *Times-Picayune*, where he
   made
A littler bibliography: *Southern Tall-Tale*
Sources. Fairly useless, he'd think;
Hence easily published, as it was.

Of greater moment were, the pillared
Moss-hung house, white, spacious, cool;
With his large room, two dollars
A day; the fungus on his shoes;
The French Quarter (proper jazz then,
Not just for tourists); the chicory
Kicking back in the throat, in all the coffee;
The streetcar where the only empty seat
Was at the back, for negroes.
Zeb took it; trouble duly came.
He hated the *verboten* then, being pro-black,
As he resents that other now, being pro-white:
Freedom the loss; issues turned round; fear just the same.

His contribution
To civilisation done,
He went to Mexico, to Monterrey,
And there is he, first day,
First morning, on the flat roof
Of small hotel. Flat city, mountains all around,
Distant, but clear, clear, intimate. Later, there'd be
A lady, cool in grey silk dress
In Sanborn's: beautiful, in part
Because not showing, because not knowing it.

Zeb spent his last night waiting
On station platform (train eight hours late);
And slowly saw it covered, every inch
With beggars, and the homeless ones.
Glimpses, fastening on memory;
But quite enough to teach him, there, and then,
That he was of an older world,
Like them.

Celibate, and happy for some eighteen months
Was Zeb. One night, at two a.m., he met
A lady from the university: large, as he liked;
Not so young; graduate student – sociology.
He sensed the end of sex-adversity,
With start of complication and perversity.
They left bar, and friends, as one; embraced, arranged
Next evening's dinner: for dessert, embraced again.
Next, she (not he) suggested taking
Her bed down from the wall;
A Murphy bed, she called it –
All prepared, neat, raking,
Ready, wrought-up, firm, and slim;
Something quite new to Zeb, and just like him.

A nice girl, closely studied;
From Baltimore (where the Browns had gone –
A heartwarming connection); she a bit blue-blooded,
Sensitive, and in Zeb's view right to be,
Caught working in a field like sociology;
A bit sore-wounded somehow, too; pleased
To keep some distance. It worked well, eased
Relations for a while; each 'phoned as fancy
Stirred: meals and things eaten, not so frequently.

Zeb came to wish they met more often, since
He (always prone to let emotions fleet
Grow to dominate – especially when on heat)
Came to feel lonely, restless, toward the end of day;
Condition not relieved in any way
By Harvard winter, by himself, a thousand miles away.
Relations, on return, were not the same:
He's grown possessive, irritable, irritating;
And, as was his way, messed up the thing.

States of beholder and beheld, the old enigma,
Threw an opaque, uncertain veil over
Zeb's year at Harvard. It should have been
A marvel: he free, on fellowship; background
Seductive: New England: Autumn: massed trees,
Gold, crimson, magenta; back to gold;
Roadside stalls of magic, blazing, beguiling,
All the colours; huge pumpkins smiling
After surgery for Hallowe'en.

Soon, winter snow looked fine against
Colonial red brick, mature; round the white board house
On Harvard Street where Zeb had his room
For ten dollars a week. From there, he could
Walk, and not so far, for all he pleased:
Library, massive, Greek, – a bit
On the chilling side. The street
Offered good drugstore food, and cheap:
The camera shop, the corner bar
Seeming frowned on by University,
Just right. When Zeb hungered
For larger, St. Louis things, he took
The subway: to Common, Filene's
Amazing basement bargains; Scollay Square,
Now slightly less disreputable than ten years back, in
      war,
But still Zeb's natural place: Old Howard
Burlesque, where old friends performed,
With sawdust on the floor. All now gone,
Swamped by high-rise depression (but this
Is not the place for lamentation).

There were the Red Sox: rich, not entirely
Efficient; but not the Browns, indeed.

109

Still, they did play the Orioles, Browns' ghosts;
Odd, cheering the visiting team. Fenway Park's
Left field wall is where home runs fly above
Like flocks of starlings. Zeb should have been
Content, and almost was, so close to pleasure-
Places. And to the times: he saw
Eisenhower's parade, down the Cambridge main street;
Stevenson, too; went to hear the speeches.
A smart young man in a blue suit
Did not speak, but was John Kennedy.

The University
Did not demand, intrude. He went to lectures;
Much like Durham, better and worse. He had
A supervisor for his dissertation – famous, indolent,
Who said, "Fine, fine," when Zeb, rarely, went
To hint at what he thought to do.
So nothing was done, for over half
The year. He had a friend
From the start: young Scots physicist,
Met on the introductory tour. Later
(Zeb then at Yale) there were visits,
Warm Christmases: the Yale football game,
Cheering opposing teams. Though Zeb
Achieved no work till time enforced, he
Was busy being busy; had part-time tasks,
Patrolled examinations at the Law School
(He should have singled out a promising
Lawyer then; that might have saved
Some trouble). All was smooth,
All take or leave, and Zeb was free –
Too free, perhaps: the place appeared to say
"You're here, at this important place
(That never needs to say so);
You may make contact, manage

110

Some small impact, passing through:
Unlikely: in the end, we'll be the same: not you."

            Zeb was
Too much the gadfly. For when time
Did run short, forcing some panic-fraught
Action, he met with giving, kindness, the warmest sort;
Dignified, keeping a distance, and none the worse
For that. Old Mr. Clarke, in the old house
On Beacon Street, gave him a top-floor room;
Access to family papers. Zeb would spend afternoons,
Sit, warm in winter, and Emerson, Thoreau, Margaret
Fuller, Channing, Cranch would talk to him
In letters: a century and more, drifting away –
Illusion old Mr. Clarke, kind, ghost-like,
Never disturbed. Zeb did some work, wrote
The dissertation thing, in six brief weeks.
Odd for him, it must have been some work
That had been missing: most things that had been
Troubled, out of tune, cohered.

            A lot given to Zeb
That year; only this end-work taken.
His own fault: walking dilemma;
Deep in commitment here, his being still
In England; and his surface heart
Still in St. Louis (sex played much part).
Longing for letters; day spoiled if they missed.
Future unknown; little he touched,
And little touched him there, saving his friend.
A mess of change; the giving at the end.

Frost had his not-taken road: now a small one for Zeb.
There he is, new Ph.D., and their first
With "Distinction," so they said.
No jobs at home. Offers from
Vassar, and the University
Of Toronto. Zeb was much inclined
Towards Vassar. Then he got
A letter: indignant, official, signed
By a real General, saying
He should have registered
For the U.S. draft. Zeb was amazed,
Replying, he'd just done six years' war
In the Raf (and on the same side).
He was forgiven, if he swore
To register should he come back for more
To the U.S. So he did, and pronto.
It did, however, hold him up so long
He had to choose Toronto.

Better not speculate upon
Where the other road-fork might have gone.
At least, one consoling thought and aid is
The Vassar scene is different now, from then,
And though it's still a honey-pot of ladies,
Mixed in among them, now, are men.

In young Zeb's time, the Mod Lang Ass,
At annual meeting
Determined what deserved anointing
In scholars' pieces (which, if not finding print,
Used to preclude appointing,
And therefore eating).

What they demanded then, persistently,
Was footnotes, long, prolix,
Germanic, military style, consistently
(Orders of Day in M.L.A. Style Sheet).
It mattered not what you wrote in your text
Or argument; what came before, or next;
That could be, often was,
A load of bolix.

Thus, what lined Toby Bolinek's cage
Those years ago, may well have bored
The bird clean off his perch.
Can he be blamed if, in his own dominion,
He reads what's there below his claws,
And passes an opinion?

But all of that's now totally corrected,
And how. Footnotes and style *passé*,
The shifting Grail is latterly directed
More towards Content – what you say;
Which is, of effort, an enormous saving.
For, now, the only rules are that you be
Correct, Politically;
And, yet more important, raving.

Now, they still meet, with papers on
"Technomuscularity and

113

The Boy Eternal": "Is Alice still
In Phallus land?"
As well as, on the roster,
"Hollywood and the Butch
Femme Fatale. A Love
Letter to Jodie Foster."

What to conclude of this progression
Between extremes, is very hard to say
(And all performed in half a century).
On balance, though, it does seem clear
That, though to bore to tears, then death, is bad,
It may be better – just – than running mad.
Now, why? Thinking's still possible, reasons broached
Why boredom sank to coma, then paralysis:
Harder to find a critical approach
To chaos, which defies analysis.

Hence, no one needs now to fear unravellers
Of feminist virago, pos. (or is it neg?) discriminators,
Post-mods, deconstructors, multiculturalists,
Lip-servers, or other academic travellers
To the cutting edge. What trick,
Trend, con, cult or embezzlement
Comes next? Who knows? But live off it
Till academe's next rave-in's fun and profit.

It was the earlier of these extremes
Zeb hoped, moving to another nation
To escape – Germanic boredom, obfuscation
In what found print, profession's expectation.
And so it proved, to some degree;
Toronto was a place where he
Could make comparisons with ten years before.
Differences vast: then moribund, the city now more
Modern, large, nearly sophisticated: bars,
Business, money, scurry. The University
An island, oldish-fashioned, British rather;
But trying to be Canadian, less like its father.

Our Dept. Head, scholar of Milton, like him remote and
    pensive;
A bachelor, dry, Mod Lang Ass in style, though less
    offensive.
But since we seemed to teach from when we rose
Till dusk, it mattered little, were we pro-
Establishment or not, since there was no time
To write at all. Teaching was fine;
Bright students, with some others; what seems
To re-occur in Zeb's more troublous dreams,
Is teaching Engineers a course
In English Lit. (compulsory). A theatre, designed
For post-mortems, Zeb the corpse;
Banks of seats, sheer, like cliffs
O'erhanging, and about to fall
On him, and full of engineers, all six feet tall
Or more; rough, scruff and spotty.
The syllabus, to instruct and entertain
Them, was poetry; and nothing but
Pope and T.S. Eliot, for weeks on end, a choice
Impossible and potty. This was where he,

115

Zeb, learned to defy adversity;
And even that had its amusing bit.
He had, and fast, to meet Canadian Lit.
E.g., to teach a novel, by one Mitchell, *Who
Has Seen the Wind?* so
Known generally as *Who Has Had the Wind?*
And that is all Zeb can recall of it.

Zeb bought his own first car:
Ancient, small, beetle-like, and blue;
The smallest car he'd ever seen, or knew
Of. He taught himself, progressively, each dawn
To circumnavigate the green collegiate lawn
Entirely in first gear, for several days;
Then second, as a later phase,
Then to the others. This process done, Zeb's
Students, showing initiative, with a little wit,
Picked up the tiny chariot; carried it
Up the grand library steps, to heights between Greek
    columns,
Thus causing Zeb to drive it down again:
Car somewhat shaken, driver tense and solemn.

For the rest, he was content
Enough; roomed on an avenue, St. George,
High up, above the trees; a daughter of the stable
Desirous, rather than desirable.
Leaving the university, exhausted, sore,
Zeb finds a cheering, chromed-prosperous
Polish about Bloor Street, and the drugstore
Where he takes pleasant meals, reads newspapers,
And as new worker, whom some, ignorant, consult,
Feels part of things, burgeoning, almost adult.

It was one of those times, unrecognised, unknown
Then, but proving crucial later:

Had he done nothing, kept the *status quo*,
The pleasant days may well have gone so
Easily on, in the same rut, for years to pass.
But all was energy, and business graspers
(Unpleasant echoes of the first-met arse-
Creepers at the *Mirror*): old hackles raised,
His judgement flew. In such a set,
A pretty girl – indeed she'd been
In the odd film in a minor way – was met;
She being shoved and edged from secretary
To something much more seamy. Zeb fell,
Needing to be rescuer, became engaged as well,
And later married her. Bloody hell, Zeb,
I know it is with hindsight that I view
Your worst decisions, but, could I get at you
With baseball bat, I'd make you hot, and rue
That one, with several others; you must have thought
A bit, about what can be done, and what cannot.

Children, they once were one, in a war.
Then parted, and for years;
Met again, once,
In the England known before.
She, now, remarried, emigrated.
Before she left for family, work, abroad,
They had tea; friendly
Enough, pleasant. He put her on the train.
Before it left, she suddenly shed tears,
Making him not the same again
For other years.

Zeb lacking, as he always has, a talent for resisting,
And having just undone his life again, was now
Nonplussed; when Fate's atoms, shifting,
Sent him by telegram a job at Yale –
A prospect, in the circs., he found uplifting.
He (nursing some affection for the States)
Returned, and gladly, grateful to the Fates.
Oddly enough, he'd been at Yale before;
Ten years ago, uniformed, in the war;
Visiting, with Polish G.I. friend, the East;
Warmly met at one college, Berkeley
(Master, then, Samuel Hemingway, since deceased).
Now, after years of flying, fun and education,
It seemed a track predestined and quite neat
To reach a college just across the street,
Branford, where Zeb became a Fellow.
You'd think ten years might have produced some mellow
Quality – something I doubt quite much:
Still light in head and foot, picaresque and such,
And altered not enough. Yale, not at all.
I said across the street: streets, here, a web
From the Old Campus, are all with colleges dotted,
Nicely worked in; trees, carved stone, baronial;
Some, seeming to blush, American Colonial.
And all is quiet, civilised, and sure.

Defining that, Zeb feels he can't do more
Than speak of Richard Sewall, one of integrity
Balanced with equanimity, to a degree
Unmet by Zeb before. Appearing insignificant,
Smallish, retiring, modest, he taught a magnificent
Course on The Tragic; his own man, bright, balanced,
    fair,
Hospitable: junior staff ever out to tea, there
At his home, and for tennis, and touch

119

Football. He was athletic, skilled; relaxed;
Could give a run to younger Zeb, then fleet,
Around a squash court. You could learn
Something towards being a man, decently,
Each time you saw him in the street.
When loss struck later in his life, tearing
To pieces, he, seeming to discount it,
Remained himself, climbed, could surmount it
Like some old Greek, defiant. It matters
Nothing, if you cease seeing, even lose
One, like that one. He teaches on, by being
Remembered. In Zeb's time (it accorded ill)
Richard was no full professor; book unfinished, to end,
Crown, a career. The book was done, and well.
It's been a state that ever seemed to draw Zeb to a friend.
Make of that what you will.

                    Teaching was always
Pleasant, there; it could be a delight.
Come now to the tiny room, high, tight,
Up in the Harkness Tower, where Branford Coll. was:
Long table; above it beams in red, blue, gold,
All medieval style, as, in imagination, old
Europe, before America became a nation:
One or two windows, outsides mere slits, insides more
    narrow,
Presumably to reduce the risks of arrows
From the Old Campus, opposite.
It was essential, just because of this,
To keep the light on always, a condition
Of symbolic sort for Zeb, starting to find
Astonishing things could happen in the mind,
Not known before.

                He had a seminar
In nineteenth century thought. Few students, and far

Better than met before. They read: they really read, so
Carlyle, Mill, Arnold, Ruskin, Newman,
Pater, and the rest, spoke, persuaded, and by book;
All of us, students, thought, struggled, waded
On, questioned, argued. Small things took
On meaning; found place in larger wholes.

Zeb, for example, thought he'd found a view
For seeing poetry (the Romantics') whole, a new condition
For him, replacing massed, dividing definitions.
What came of that, years on (I will be terse!),
Was understanding how, later, in Arnold's verse,
Internal dynamics (forgive the language!) work
To keep it poetry, active, moving, still alive; though sad,
Paralysed, in content. (I'll leave that here – I heard you
    wince;
But, some time, read the stuff and texts, and be convinced
Or not, just as you wish.) Later on, Zeb, no longer the
    young Turk
But still excited, thought some things might be said of
    Wordsworth's work,
Even now. Among them, that *The Thorn,*
Which usually occasions merely yawns
If read at all, within or out of season,
Is quite a marvellous poem: Zeb gave his reasons.
Again, see what you think; I know
What I do.

It's time, in case he gets to more ideas, and other,
To pass from that small room, and find another,
Be it drab, steam-heated boiling hot
At eight a.m. He teaches there, remedial work to students
    not
Quite up to scratch. It still was fun. Two students that
Were not the best even there (I'm not sure if they passed)
Sought out Zeb's flat; presented an umbrella, one so slim,

121

A surprise present they had bought for him.
It turned into a walking stick, using its silk
Collapsing cover: costing as much
From some expensive Ivy League emporium
As Zeb's whole monthly pay. Touched,
He's never dared bring out the *parapluie*,
But soon will need the stick, supportively.

Before we leave dull matters academic,
Zeb noticed it was common, even endemic
To find bright students seeming, as a rule,
To have emerged ungrounded from their school
In simple things like punctuation, spelling,
Forming a sentence. Drawn by such schools, he soon
Found they packed up, locally, each early afternoon,
Among other things. In short, and without elation,
He actually grew interested in education;
Wrote a piece in *Harper's*, and was paid
What seemed a lot of money, then.
Recall, this was the 'Fifties: schools selective
In British nation, universities too; soon suffering elective
Shifts: education, in days shortly to come, handed
To Shirley Williams: all then much expanded
In order that miseducation reach
All; lives adjusted, comprehensively,
Each having right to ignorance, democratically.

It's best to leave foreshadows, and to end
On Saturdays; out to the Yale Bowl, wend
Your way. Sunshine, champagne on picnic tables
By station-wagons; the day so blue
And clear, you see for miles; trees gold
And red; crowd huge, game close;
McGill, or other hero, running just past all hope,
Settling it, so near its end. That seems
The sort of memory with which to leave – unchanging.

122

Zeb's fellows, all inbred, felt, ever, dread
Of leaving: he, the stranger, still free in his head.
If you think he idealises, turns fair to best,
Recall he's on the young side still, thoughts bent out West
For something new. Let what's complete, unmarred, end
With grace; part easily. Take the gift, leave
Something behind, as friend.

In Alabama
The farmer let us park,
Sleep, on his land;
Invited us to supper.
He said he had no prejudice,
Got on well with the coloureds.
Why, some of their kids, he said,
Were real cute.

Zeb, who knew so little then,
Was dutifully appalled
At the condescension.

Now, a bit further on, and mended,
He's merely grateful for the warmth,
Genuine enough, that was intended.

A long drive, through mountains
Up to twelve thousand feet: snow, cloud, cold;
Then down to desert and the coast;
Five hundred miles in the day;
Late evening into Mazatlan.
Only one collapsing small hotel, dirty,
Rough, hot. He washed,
Looked at his wife, on the bed, sleeping,
Exhausted, covered in sweat;
Both knowing there was little left
Between them. Then he saw,
About to crawl on to the sleeping face,
A two-inch cockroach from the filthy floor;
Just in time, he lifted it, took it out,
And never said.

But he, sudden, knew
That she was there, in this awful place,
Only because of him. Nothing large
Was changed, or came of it: but the moment
Of all those others in ten thousand miles,
With other months and years,
Has stayed – against each not knowing
Where the other is, now, if still alive.
Some odd trick of the memory, selecting
The moment still there, valued, part
Of himself, of her. Connecting.

From the mountains' thick mist, dulling
All, down to Gauguin jungle and road
Private, trafficless, ceaselessly creeping
Through greenness; hot, wet-sultry, lulling
Car and man to trance, almost to sleep.
Round the bend, taken widely, sudden,
Coiled, soaking the sun in, was placed
A great snake.

Blurred-yellow in hot light, thick,
Thick coils tumbled, piled high on the road;
He felt me coming, tried to move.
No time: no time for him
Nor me: one thud, turning the stomach,
Battering the heart; softening, later,
To fury-sorrow, then self-hate;
Or hate of the thing done, perpetrated.

But he moved! He did! – still, somehow,
Moved himself, and quite some way
Off the road, and sun,
Into the green, and shade.

Better perhaps, to be dead, coloured as clay
As he was,
And I to have killed him,
Than not to be able to say.

Destiny, shaping our ends, makes thin and fat ones,
A bit like Science: energy shifts atoms
Here, then there, like chess pieces, in patterns.

So, in the 'Fifties ('Sixties too), Zeb had some chances,
Events, adventures; separate romances
Which in hindsight cohere, as in gavotte-like dances.

They join, as if magnetically attracted
Together: meaning not to be extracted,
Unless it was: they seem to have been subtracted

Or postponed, from his youth: rescheduled to fall
Later; Zeb now free, on leash extended, or no leash at all
Or current wife not there, or even agreeable.

Zeb drove, like Lochinvar, out of the West, most
   celebraty;
Then flew, for thirteen hours, in free-drinks bar, all matey;
Or took a ship, apt haunt for the uncelibaty.

However it was, odd things, a trick or
Two, do drift together here. They ask to stick a
Name on them; so, call them *Transatlantica*.

It sounds no more than halfway to adventure, now,
To have driven, then, across the States,
Before the tourists ran their races
Seeding, everywhere, the commonplaces.
Zeb crossed, returned, re-crossed, again, again.
From all the miles and years
Remain alive only the long straight roads
In the West; the slow build-up
Of sweat as a day moved. Las Vegas
(Food free or cheap), but nothing else
Real enough to get hold of. Perhaps
Eddie Fisher and a night-club meal
For twelve dollars; Zeb noting,
As she left stage, the Eliz. Taylor
Legs were not as might reasonably
Have been expected. Reno, Salt Lake
City; then slower change over the days.
More road signs, more often, more complex;
Wariness, more people, West to East.
Motels that looked good (then not sold with sex
Films); hamburgers, Howard Johnsons, drinks,
Heat. Four hundred miles a day
To the new town, new place, new evening;
The sweaty, spurious sense of achievement;
Tired to bed. All clicked together: days
Into a new half-reality; one dimension away, precisely.

What splits one trip from the rest
For Zeb, was finding messages
At friends' spaced across continent, to ring
The wife who'd left, and was remarrying;
An evening cry of pain at every stop,
And growing. She was in pain, and worse;
Nostalgic, longing, lost. He must explain.

128

You can't go back, undo, reverse
The patterns. But the pain shared
Became his also, in perpetuity; and though
It's likely now, each thinks the other
Dead, some pain remains, relates;
Soured first, then dimming change,
Escape, half-adventure, driving across the States.

There he is, in his thirties now,
A slight case of postponed development.
Free, free. Straight off the ship, sent
Out charged up with six days' boredom.
Here, and free. The hired Jaguar
Is old, classic. He drives from Plymouth
Through greening lanes unseen before;
Arrives, to see an old connection
From the 'forties: comfortable, mature;
But he holds off. How can I know why?
Just one more mystery – what Zeb might do
And does not, why should I understand? I merely sigh.

He's taken in to see
Her daughter, who's in bed, lush, seventeen.
What do you make of that? Zeb does not
Seem to know: is it some grotesque sadism,
Re-run of paralysing twins, his landladies
In Sale, from twelve years ago?
He tries to sort it out; confused, preoccupied, half
Unavailable to Mother's romp.
Then she gets in his car; turns round,
Seeming to sit on the gearshift – what
Does go on? – she missed: a flounce
Of skirt, a gasping, then a veering;
Zeb surprised, deftly astounded, taken
At point of no return, and of no steering.
He'd never thought that he could be
Caught in uncertainty, seduced – seduced nothing,
Raped; and nothing to be done
But the set motions,
Struggling towards control, wondering
Where the fault is.

The old joke comes: lean back,
Enjoy it. Does he now know
What assault is?

All travel's pre-imagined, made
Of hope, half-expectation, or less; both
Built-in magnifiers. When the timing once
Is wrong, a mere flat evening
Looms large, is fadeless,
Altering the scale, for memory.
There's at least some philosophic scope
To rock bottom.

Take one evening: London, in the 'fifties.
Nothing wrong (for a few more years)
With the setting, at least.
Zeb, new-arrived. Raf sort
Of drinking club; drinkers, new-met;
Some girls, the un-kind; so
Precariously balanced: amateur-pro,
Courtesan-independent, brassy-attractive;
Suggesting a Peggy Lee show
In some Piccadilly club, if the men
Would buy the tickets.

            Show and singer
Too skilful, hard, polished brass.
Zeb's paired girl more so;
Breathes in suspicion, exhales
Tensions, resentments. Zeb shy,
Unsure; hated progressively for it.
Future, cheapened London to come
Is here crushed into prophecy.

Zeb, why do you
Travel at all? Why come
Here, now? It cannot solely be
That you can think of no alternative.

132

Is this the start
Of a visit, held in the mind
For a year? – its worst wounding,
Logicless, scarring memory
For decades?

You never knew exactly what
A charter flight would be.
This one paused in Iceland:
Sky bluer blue, earth brown, bare;
All clear as ice; so stark, faintly
Frightening; making past solidities
Shadows. In the air
Thirteen hours, we sat upstairs, as
In a flying boat: long oval room,
We seated round its walls: the centre was
A bar, busy, alive; dispensing
Free drinks; no limits, no let
Or hindrance.

        Next to Zeb
Was Liselotte: New York, Jewish, friendly;
Half cynic, half enthusiast. Shapely; a fullness
Well grouped. The intelligence of privilege,
Sophisticated; liberal finish, by Sarah Lawrence.
Calm talk, polite; then interesting,
Libricated. Then a reaching, meeting;
A letting go. At midnight, they
Brought blankets round. Better
Put two together, and share. Lights out;
Eyes cancelled: adventure is exploration;
Is of touch, supposing, imagining, hoping;
Seeking, and to find. You can't
Eliminate sound, muffle awareness.
When the light came, it slowly showed
As stars come out, a hundred eyes,
Half accusing, jaundiced, zealous,
Overhung, bleared. Zeb thought, jealous.

He went with her to her hotel.
But, this was the 'fifties; he was told,
And gravely, it would not be possible
To see the lady in her room.
Only in the lounge, Sir.

It did lead on, unevenly, as
These things go. Meetings, old York,
Then New: fringe politics, even
Meetings with family; Zeb's status undiscussed.
A good kid, Liselotte; honest. Correcting
Zeb, once: "I'm not your girlfriend –
I'm your mistress." Charter flights,
As I said, can bring
The unexpected.

NINETEEN SIXTIES

Do not think the tiny abcess, festering,
Built of a thousand fears from novels,
Then met in life, sinking the heart,
Is merely of the New World, where
Things are larger, stark. It is
Of the Epoch, of things to come;
Things I shall leave to lie in wait
For you. Now a flowing poison, well beyond
The damming up: then, no more
Than the small sad hint, needing to be read.
Consider, then let this be interpreted.

        Zeb, full of holiday,
Went to a dance: the old Assembly Rooms
In York. A few drinks first:
Jazz dancing, warmth, sweat. At one o'clock
They leave: Zeb, solicitor friend and wife,
Ex-Raf friend and wife – five. Zeb drives them
To his host's in his old U.S. Rambler car. Gaiety;
Much talk; no traffic; he gets
Road directions a bit late, makes
Two sharp turns, a bit late too;
They arrive. Before they leave the car,
Policeman's head is at the window, sudden, like
Magic. Zeb winds it down; police jaw drops
A moment, then: "We don't like the way
You were driving." Zeb, with lawyer friend,
Is taken to police station. A contest
Starts: relaxation (drink?), with some
Polysyllabic words (ten times more power
To raise constabulary ire, than swearing) on the one hand;
Mounting police fury on the other.

It lasts four hours. First, the Sergeant

139

Tries to stop Zeb speaking to his solicitor
Alone. Then, an order: Zeb is to turn out
His pockets. Lawyer refuses
On his behalf. Police: – "He might have a knife,
Or commit suicide in the cells." This failing,
They say it is a new directive; asked to
Produce it, they cannot. Zeb is examined
By a doctor (police again attempt to keep
His lawyer out). Examination is pleasant:
Chat about universities, rugby.
The little comedy plays on: a sixpence
Is put on the floor; Zeb is to
Pick it up; he does, with ease, some grace; puts it back
On the floor, where the sergeant simply cannot
Get his fingers round it. No one laughs.
Zeb is told a charge of drunk driving
Cannot be made. Police drive him
And friend home. Zeb notices, and lawyer
Points out, that the police driver
Is exceeding the speed limit. "Just trying
To get you home, Sir."

That should have been
The end of it. Next day
Zeb and friend go to football – well, if not football,
To watch York City play. There, on duty
Is the small, peppery police Inspector
From last night. "Good afternoon, Officer,"
Says lawyer friend. Effects, spectacular:
A B-movie in excess. The small round face
Set round the waxed moustache, grew
Red – a real red, crimson; moustache seems
To fade as contrast changes, white to puce;
Mucus, then foam began to dribble, loose
From the lips. Explosion threatened; memories
Twenty years old, stirred: Corporal Stuckey

140

As shrunken grotesque-ghost. They
Moved on, knowing this was not
The end of it.

Days passed. Then a charge was made:
Dangerous Driving, carrying a sentence
Of four months' prison; meaning, for Zeb,
No return abroad, and loss of job.
The Court met. The police account
Outran belief. But one young constable,
Inexperienced, who rode in the police-car,
Told the truth – God help his career!
Magistrates, without leaving the courtroom,
Dismissed the case.

Zeb didn't let it go. He sent
A report to the Home Office,
Who ordered an enquiry.
It was held by the York Police (yes!)
Who found: There was no need
For further action.

Two weeks before, a magistrate in York
Had passed cars stopped at
A pedestrian crossing; driven over it;
Hit a boy on the crossing, carried him
Sixty feet, causing serious head injuries.
He was charged with Driving without
Due Care and Attention; fined
Fifteen pounds. (Remember,
Zeb, no accident, no contact,
Was charged with Dangerous
Driving, criminal – if guilty, four months.)

Police enquiries concluded
That such comparisons would be

Improper. Zeb knows now
The only place to go to was the press.
He didn't; soured enough with them, before.

What was the motive? Zeb's theory
Is: all was directed at his lawyer
Friend, whose job was often to defend against police
Prosecutions. Recall, how the constable's
Jaw dropped, as he looked into the car
To complain of the driving? It was
A left-hand drive, and his moment
Of astonishment came from seeing early
The steering wheel within Zeb's hands,
The quarry over in the passenger seat.
At least, so Zeb guesses, guesses merely.

                    More important:
If you think, what a minor incident
To take so many words,
And no harm done, consider:
This was nineteen-sixty-one;
The door just slightly open.
Think, how far along that corridor
We are now.
And still travelling.

Zeb stayed, as lodger, with the mother
Of old school friend. Co-lodger,
Distant, neat-slim, cool almost to
The inimical: pretty, groomed, correct,
The young teacher of French, at the high school.
For weeks, paths hardly crossed. You could
Almost suspect dislike.

On impulse, he suggested
A meal. It turned out to be
One of those evenings that accelerate
Into new rhythm; idealise, create,
Leave nothing ordinary. All moved;
Generated its own energy, and
Fast. In the end, there she would stand
Outside her room (landlady snores, expressing
Safety). All's wordless: perfect legs, with feet
In tasteful, conservative court shoes, placed
Carefully apart, for ease of climb and access:
Frantic reachings, wrestlings in agreement
And desire. Later, only the car as haven,
As sea waves climbed in the storm outside,
Rocking. (Fate can be the hammiest
Director of B-movies.) Zeb was warmly received,
Approved, by family. Journeys, hotels;
He drove her once to London, stopping at
Some small town inn. She, having confessed to
A fiancé, had to telephone him:
An overnight delay, reluctantly enforced
By car trouble. Arrived next day, Zeb,
At farthest northern fringe of the city,
Was introduced to bristling Suspicion,
But correct. Suspicion inspected radiator, minutely;
And Zeb's lovely, loyal old Rambler

143

Dripped a few small drops,
Dutifully.

It was considerably later, when she
Made a minor revision.
He wasn't exactly her fiancé;
Rather, husband. But, she intimated,
A bit of a drip, and boring.

The names have taken on romance
Now. The *Empresses*
Of *Scotland, Canada*; the *France*.
It's probably the duller factory drills
Of the air age, that take the thanks
For that. Yet sea voyages, then, were blanks
For Zeb. Deck chairs, set manners, set pretence;
Beef tea at eleven; ship's newspaper,
Raffle, races, sea, sea, Tannoy; meals
Metronome-like, timestones marking days.
Always some special live one to avoid: he, French-
    Canadian,
Life-of-party, huge lumberjack, small moustache,
Check shirt, loud booming voice, ways
Carefully moulded for irresistibility;
Routine, routine; six days
Out of this world.

When the world came back,
It made imagined squalor
Immediate. At the New York docks
You waited with your trunks.
Up he'd come, a cliché from short story.
Surly-sidling, the amateur gangster mocks,
With his official hat, and Customs badge.
"I could do these next, in no time;" –
Hand held out, low, by the thigh,
Carelessly (this slightly surreptitious vice);
Ten dollars gets them done next; thirty
Puts them through uninspected, in a trice.
Then the cab, heat, city;
Home again, in West Corruption.
(Much cleaned up now, to take
To the airports. Ships docked

145

In history.) What happens
To corruption's energies, its atoms,
When place and time
Dictate change?

The Raf made varied friendships.
You came to know the one, or two
To last. The indestructible
Creeps up; drops disguises. At one moment
Given, certainty, you find,
Has crept into the mind.

Past times, distant laughter, transmute
To loyalties; go on. The night the two
Of you have a date, with twins from down the road.
Just pretty girls; younger, far, embarrassingly.
Then all takes off, ignites
Into the memorable. Exuberance
Is when you know, inside, at that
One second, that vignette is statuette, to be
Carved, life long, in memory. Outside,
No more than jokes, fun, stories bubbling up; heights
Of invention, thought impossible; laughter; closeness.
The miracle of inhibitions gone, replaced
By simple happiness.

                    If you want
To be technical, not much
Went on. Car ride, a few inches
Of tongues down throats. A sense
Of something so well achieved, not quite
Believed; perfect, itself
Stolen from everyday. Gone,
But a legacy, shared, on, on
Between friends.

Friends enjoy still
Arsenal nil, Ipswich nil,
And dull, dull; because

147

They laugh at it
Together.

The atoms, forces
Are never still. Magnets
Change, move; iron filings
Shift patterns. One
Moves to the domestic, veers back:
One, more alone, turns inward to that.
The patterns change: to attract
Is power to repel.
Shadows of living: death; dread; escape. Well
To grip to something. Set courses change even rocks;
Winds force it. It's memory that mocks,
Or is mocked.

New fork in the road: new work,
New town, state, sea; far edge
Of a continent. Old adventure, war,
Hollywood and the rest, of fifteen years before,
Made new again. Leave Yale, and Ivyness,
Friends; turn car, possessions, West.
Some small new frontiersman; new journey
To new life. Take time, intensify;
Drive, not West direct, but South, by
San Antonio, Monterrey, sun,
Mountain, desert; Mexico City, on
To Taxco, Guadalajara, up the coast;
Nogales; California. Twelve
Thousand miles, to newness.

What stays? A little here, more there.
In Nogales put the wife to bed;
Take a caleche, trot in cooler air
To night explorings, past-desperate as old,
But new, here. It all comes down
To moments, chosen, mind-pressed
As real. A few miles into desert, park on sand, put
Insect screens on car windows, flatten back
As usual, seats into beds, comfortless.
Lie side by side, listening
To desert sounds, music pulsating
On instruments alive, unknown, maddened out there
With force. We, waiting for desert air
To cool. It never does. We leave
At five a.m.; sick of tossing, sweat;
Trying, thinking, trying to sleep,
Failing. The cost of a motel
Saved. An early start, to sweep
Over the last desert, mountains, then

149

Canyons: something given, to keep.
This English girl, strange in this place,
This heat, this force, herself bewildered
At her own first small steps in beauty's loss:
You knew, she knew she could have had
Things, money, dominance, whatever
It is they want; could have played
The game to win, and more directly.
Now troubled by rocks driven between
Them; yet, without complaint, stayed,
Suffering the rough, petty economies
Still to be with Zeb. How should
She know, that he took something, sent,
Of value in that dawning of acknowledgement?
A thing for the years
Of trouble, shifting,
Parting; a thing that touched, then,
Some life-nerve. What stopped its telling?
The law that, in the doomed moment
Of losing, knowing
Comes of what's been given
Precisely as it's going;
As the small household felt
Its way through last dawn canyons, by
Mists, down to Riverside,
Where the river's dry.

Zeb was talked into playing
First Voice: *Under Milk Wood.*
A bit too slow, and too deliberate, he
Chewed word-sounds, self-indulgently.
Hearing it now, he'd like to wind
His spring up tighter, if he could.
A little reached across, connected; created
Response; the cameraderie, the thing made,
Done; the spell of words elated;
Evenings saved; some harmony, some giving.
Some focus, heightening the living.

I

Huge, Welsh, friendly, gregarious,
With gift of gab from some Welsh Blarney Stone,
He taught Classics; no Ph.D.; prospects precarious.
Axe duly fell; back to his Celtic home.
Would Zeb help pack a few things, Man?
Saturday lunch: time to go,
Pack, take the stuff to San Pedro,
To the ship, its deadline set
For noon (which was when packers,
Zeb and Duff Thomas, met).

A tiny pile of firewood sticks
Each smaller, far, than a foot rule
Lay on the kitchen floor
By a gigantic 'frig, latest,
Whitest, largest of devices, many
Unsuited to Welsh current,
If any.
Packing construction to be led
By Zeb, Duff said: that was the plan:
A hammer; eight, even nine, nails.
"What's the first move," he said,
"Then, Man?"

Hours passed. Monster manhandled, then,
Into the station-wagon; the 'frig as white, as menacing,
As nude, as it was born. At four p.m.,
Sun belting down, clad just in shorts, shoes, socks,
They set out for L.A.; arrived by six;
Asked their way, tortuous, to the docks.
Closed, barbed wire enclosed, locked then
For weekend; ship to sail at p.m., ten.

What happened then is
On loaves and fishes scale.
He found a caretaker,
Prised him from his feed,
And talked: the Welshness lilted
On. The man agreed
To take it in, pack it in proper padding;
Put it on the ship, addressed. No cash
Changed hands, though Zeb did think
The man about to tip Duff
Or himself, being so pleased to do
All he could – a privilege, he said.

With other current, and in other air
Perhaps the 'frig would work all right,
If Duff talked to it
When it got there.

Duff had been Soccer Coach,
Along with Greek and Latin, tongues and tales.
In gratitude for help in packing, Man,
He left the job (unpaid) to Zeb, and ran
To Wales.

Zeb, though he loved, and loves, the sport,
Had played it once, when he was seven,
And had been lost; and once again, at twelve.
His players now, American, lads keen and fit,
Consolingly, knew less than Zeb of it.
First season: hopeless. All games lost
But one. Zeb struggled on, ever, ever
Repeating basics: lads began, faintly, to prosper,
To be a team. Season two: unreckoned,
Unrecognised, they finished second;
And that to U.C.L.A., whose team consisted
Of Europeans, South Americans, and knew whereof it
    did.
Zeb voted Coach of Year in S. Cal. Soccer League,
Knowing that, over in Wales, Duff must have talked to
    God:
Choice Blarney words, a few
At least. Hence Miracle Two.

The Third awaited yet.
It had not been divulged: all would expect
The Coach to raise a donnish team, select,
To play his charges – these strong, half-skilled now, also
   young.
Zeb had to play, himself. Ineffectual, tongue
Hanging like a dog's; aged forty years, Zeb
(Not the dog) was set to fall on lovely earth
And die, when the ball arrived. He kicked
It vaguely up the middle, past halfway line, ran,
Caught it up: no one to pass to; only four steps
Left in him; then, all breath, all life would stop.
He ran three, kicked, stood; the ball
Rose in a lovely arc, then drifted left;
'Keeper advanced, easily, to take it, but it swerved
Nicely to the top corner of the net, so deft;
So beyond credence, and all minds.
Life flooded back to Zeb, now mended.
Invention, too: to act as if all were intended.
He put a fresh look on, as if finding it
A bit too elementary; took himself off. Well done, Man,
Said the Welsh voice in his brain.
Grateful, he never kicked a serious ball again.

In theory,
Saluting knowledge,
Authority, elective,
May take tax cash,
Start a college, selective
Of teachers; pay them well;
Admit only the brightest
It can find.
Curriculum: best books. Sell
Out to no one; be
A public Ivy League;
New classic Greece, as well;
Temple, to Mind.

Zeb's been rehearsed
In three such trials;
Lasting a year, a mile
Or two, then turned
By Change, and, worse,
The Meaningful kind.
Which simply means
Each social fad
Gets its Sub-Deans,
As flows new Isis
To Budget Crisis.

More students required, brain
Optional. More conquers less.
More buildings, titles, deans, donations,
More print, enterprise, public relations.
Less reaching, and more mindlessness.
College of Mind now

University of More.
Turnover, that of
Any whore.

A local result of the above
Was the arrival of a Scholar
From the Midwest; stamped Approved, Fit,
By Mod Lang Ass,
With acres of print
On American Lit.,
To sort out the Dept.
And all within it.

All once more divided
Into Creepers (Reliants),
And Others (Defiants).
Zeb felt it becoming a bit of a bore,
All the times he'd viewed the scene before;
It seemed like a score; or maybe more.
He must give a paper, on a book not yet dreamed.
At its merciful end, the New Master's eyes gleamed;
He ran up to Zeb, said "Superb!" – seized his hand;
A clear invitation to join Creepers' band.
There was some gain: several had learned,
Had seen the depth of fraud confirmed.
They soon left, those who could.
And Lo! bow heads, to see
Reconstituted, near-new English Dept.,
Made, largely, of new wood
From the Conforming Tree.

It had been expected.
Now, she's actually gone.
He ought to feel desolate, sad
At least at loss of the familiar;
Or even some excitement at the new.
There had been chances, some, around;
Not taken up; half-surprisingly;
Now, they would not be.
Was it new conscience, inertia, or that he
Had lost something, some spark within, unknown?
Or just the new delight of choosing.
Acting, or not: or, for some reason, joy in refusing?

Now, at the leaving,
No exultation, no relief, pain or demise.
Just this spare room, bed; wish to stay, not rise.
The head turned to the side
Unmoving, numb, the mind
Filled with nothing but
Wallpaper pattern, entering the eyes
Three feet away.
Behind the head, unseen, but known,
Curtained off, great piles of things owned,
To be sorted,
Kept, sent away
Some day.

Take the ironic name, the Freeway,
Into downtown L.A.;
Slip neatly in the chosen lane
Of seven; stay.
Marvel at driving disciplines: so sane;
Forgetting easily that all those shades
Who passed, cut in to overtake
By habit, are green plots, statistics now;
Passed on, for overriding one last time
Warnings, in Calif.'s Good Rules Book
Of Driving.

                Fifty minutes gone
In concentration, akin to meditation;
Glad to be alive, alone,
You park. All's loud;
Larger, a bit, than life: the garish crowd,
Cinemas (sleaze and legit.), shops, sun, palms
In Pershing Square. These El Dorado arms
Reached out, to all of these:
Not quite assimilated, not yet cohered;
Still slightly restive, on the move;
Planted on surfaces, bright in colours, tones,
But tremulous, vulnerable: "Where you from?"
Planted, still only half-hardy
Rootless ones.

Towards evening, drive out
On Sunset Boulevard, exactly at that time
First neons wink; palms pose black
Against an orange sky. Sit, early on, in spacious
Night club, all silk and lights; have drinks
Served, by friendly waitresses.
Watch genuinely pretty girls,

160

To cheering orchestration, divesting.
All is straightforward, relaxed:
No approaches, pressures, cons, tricks, testing
To nerves; no interferences. Dances
Verging on moments' beauty; quiet trance.
What's gone regretted, even longed for;
What follows, unsurpassed, and more.
Then, you can stroll next door,
Eat a huge hamburger and fries,
Watch night gather, lights dominate, jostlings
Of the dark begin: moonrise.

It takes a lot of stick, L.A.,
A lot of snidery, for naïveté.
They say it cannot hold a candle to
The 'Stick Park, and the rest, in San Francisco.
Zeb disagrees; knowing that then,
For him, behind the eyes,
It had a power to beckon, calm:
Civilise.

I

He drove to Berkeley,
In a State car,
Four hundred miles;
For some committee thing
On student literacy
Or its lack,
Or something.

In San Francisco,
At a corner, at one or two a.m.
He went for a drink
In a well-lit bar.
It only served milk drinks:
Some fad,
Legal or trendy.
It was the Sixties.

Then a girl (of many),
Full bodied, good-
Looking enough,
Asked to buy him a drink.

It was all odd,
Unnatural;
And he, not used
To the new, vice-versa
Years, muttered excuse
And – she still protesting – left.

Missing for ever
Whatever it was.
Or could have been.

Moving along the country road
At a reasonable pace;
The mirror showed
One car behind, and driven by
The old mix, old case,
Seen (suitably) by glimpses;
Now near, now far,
Good face, the long straight hair,
Young, knowable, entirely pleasant.
Clear, unclear; half vision
Framed, portrait, then farther silhouette
Coming and going, over some miles.

To go on thus would be trance,
Contentment. The traffic circle loomed
With three exits: one chance in three she'd still
Be there. When he looked to see,
She had changed to glass, road; bare, increasing;
The circle retreating, into the past.
She, another, who will not return.

In Paris, where you expect such things
(And Zeb had years of boulevard exploration),
One girl, dark, beautiful, dressed
Formally, and to perfection: black suit, long skirt
And Longchamps hat.

Moving along the boulevard, with
Assurance, grace as Zeb had never (looking for years)
Seen, or imagined. Is beauty made to move
A beauty further, by certainty of itself, to tears?
Crowds parted, made way;
He saw them, as she walked.
She knew she lit the day
Increasingly, as evening fell, and loved it.

She stopped, to converse
Briefly, then moved on,
To meet Zeb's eye.
He could not comprehend, nor half-believe
What she was. He ran.
Then, knowing nothing, not how he moved
Entranced, returned, to sate his sight.

She glided, gently, imperiously
Circling, suggesting the whirlpool
Drawing, drawing
By the cafés, knowing-wise
To others, playing them on the line
Into the net. Each movement neat,
Calculated, beautiful, a perfect, perfect dance
Motion: the ballet on the street.

Hours melted: he could not see enough,
Ever. Drawn, drawn in, played with, near lost
He walked forward, condemned, to be claimed,
Exactly as she paused to speak
With some bedimmèd sister,
And smooth (ballet, ballet!) a stocking
Slightly above the knee.
Then, quite as if mortal,
She lit a cigarette;
And Zeb, lost, lost beyond any hope
Was sudden-free; tore for the Métro
At l'Opéra, grateful and dismembered
At once; shaken, as he is still.

Zeb could leave his small white
House, climb in his old white car,
Drive easily, see all as new, all little shocks
Of interest, set in sand, desert, space. Pause
In San Diego, especially the docks.
Drive on, so fleetingly,
To jostling line-ups of disorder
For immigration laws;
Desultory check-ups on the border
To the hot seedy chaos
On the other side. Tijuana:
Girls and bars and drinks and clubs;
Sex, hanging, hinting on the air;
With silver, sombrero hats, tooled leather goods,
All gaudy, but alive with some rare
Force. Not much ill in it all
If you had moderate sanity;
Zeb might have dropped his guard
Just once, or twice; with no harm done
Except to vanity.

Should you desire cheap luxury, space, and sun, and sea,
You could drive on, through canyons, watch the ocean
To Ensenada; a winding, sunny way
(Now obsolete, Zeb's told, replaced by super-road,
Packed with unceasing anger, fumes, and motion).
But then, it was a quiet place,
Ensenada: some fishing, just for a living;
Decent motels, in inlets from the beach;
Astounding French (for some reason) restaurants giving
Surprise and taste and cheerfulness: all
A quiet sunny pleasure, quite withdrawn
From everyday, unchanging, just short of boring.
Soon to change, as all things must;

166

But, then, reassuring;
Restoring.

You may recall that Zeb was free
Much of this phase of life;
Free, then more free, unburdened with a wife.
Surprising, then, he went to these delights
Less often, far, than you would guess:
Which puzzled him, as time went on,
And puzzles me, as much as him: no less.
He could, for certain, go, act, spend, cavort
Just as he chose; and did not, at all
Frequently, and if he did, decreasingly.
Was it maturity
At last? I know him well, by now;
And that's not it: more likely far to be
Age, with its first chemistry
Experiments. A hint or two,
First prescient intimation
Of Mortality.

Dear Old Mort,
Quiet American;
Mild, silver-haired; good sort,
Ex- Dept. Head, now replaced, forced
Out by the New Order.
A bit hurt, worried; as well as new-divorced;
Alone – first time for years,
In his small square block
Campus house; one of scores:
Flat roofs, stuccoed white against the heat,
Set out along the lawns by campus roads, all neat,
Identical: a mass of little privacies
At dollars seventy-five
Per four weeks
(Including maintenance).
Zeb, also free, in copy-house
Some way away; after the day,
Would drop in for drinks and laughter.
This evening Mort, as ever diffident,
Had a slight shamefacedness, extra unrest,
A doubt whether to tell.
He did: confessed.

He had come home, at five,
For the long sunshine evening.
Tired; made himself a drink,
Sat in his chair, and dozed: woke
Drowsy-lost; leapt with panic, horror, pain.
Half past seven: night gone; a class
Waiting for him at eight a.m. again;
Shaved (not too much growth
For a whole day); grabbed notes
With a piece of bread; skimmed
A few key phrases; briefcase seized;

168

Dashed for the door. Too late
To walk; too late to call
A cab. Down the long path, ran his race
With time, all panic, mess, and pace.
He thought somehow the sun
Shone a strange gold, in a strange place.
He paused for necessary breath:
Was this dream-fantasy, a first doorway to death?

Half-awareness grew, slow, struggling, striving
All out of place. It was
The previous evening, Zeb just arriving
For drinks, dinner, and to laugh.
A deeper gold, that evening, the last rays
Of the sun: long spell, to night and stars;
While Zeb again, again, could not hold back, control
His laughter muscles, past exhaustion, tender,
To ache for days.

They must have been surprised,
The twenty *peons*,
Hacking at cactus,
Where a road snaked through
The desert, where sun glared
Shadowless. Hours of sun:
The wide-brimmed hats nodding
All silent in the drowsy oven,
As the machetes moved
Along the hours.

          Heavy heat, and nothing.
Then nothing ripped open by the smoke,
The scream, of burning tires. The great
Green Gringo Oldsmobile tearing through space
Where cars, or any things, were rare –
At eighty m.p.h., stopped as if the air
Were concrete; still, in twenty yards;
All dimmed in dust.
When cleared, it showed
The great green painted thing
There, sudden, on the road;
Two rear-seat friends, bruised, confused.

Then sun again: twenty *peons*, fingers
To heads; twenty Latin shrugs –
Gringos, mad, as usual,
But no big deal.
Zeb, unused to automatic
Cars, tearing through hot air
And told to slow, pushed power-brake
Where clutch should be; no gears

170

Here; but a little, brighter moment
For twenty *peons*, slapping at cactus
In endless desert hours and years.

Free, life simple. Independent
Again. No, there is no missing.
Zeb's home, in his small house; a lease
On Peace: evenings of peace.
He's house-proud, too:
A little place, but tasteful.
He can go through
To Mexico, dive into crowds,
Just when he fancies;
But does not; free
Not to bother, indolently,
With anything, but being free.
And, after nearly forty years,
Home, and at his ease.

Caution, Zeb. You've reached
Havens before; thrown them away.
Never commit that error, please, O Please,
Again. I trust you more; be
Deserving of it. Enjoy
The simple things, simplicity.

The evening brings a knock upon his door:
A student, one of the mixed-up ones,
Hating, resenting, lost, inclined to loving,
Full of breast, bearing a rose.
Imagine – a young girl brings a rose
For Zeb, self-sufficient, forty, in his house.
And he succeeded in resisting.
Well done, old Zeb, for once
Doing the right thing.

It was the later knock
That brought catastrophe.

172

It was, I fear, predictable
That youth now might affect his chemistry;
Because receding youth invites recapture
By means of youth in others, inciting rapture
As its lure. It did: young girl,
Twenty, fresh-faced, nubile, pretty, and there;
Witty, and bright; and with long blonde hair
In braids.

And yet, I think, that he could still
Have kept his distance and control
Even on this occasion, timed so ill,
But for one crucial thing:
She had three dogs,
Three lovely, loving, funny, lively dogs;
And that, with all the other,
Proved too much;
Zeb gone, again,
Unable to recover.

MacSwine, this is the point, a turning
Where I'd detach from you, sever
Completely; lose all interest; let you stew forever
In your own mindless juice, unlearning.
And, as it is, I may.
It's just that – well, just that dogs
Returned again, some decades on;
Made life again quite new
For me, as well as you.
I sigh, and try,
But cannot curse, abandon, or attack
One who brought dogs back.

There the Fool fools again, steeped in affection,
Mostly his own. The dogs, happy
Making happiness, winding
Their spells of love; unique
Because unregrettable; novel
To Zeb. All lived, content,
In the small house, at reasonable rent,
That hugged the bare hillside; its view
Over the desert, where Zeb walked the dogs,
And loved the place, for they did, too.
And she – she was the extrovert he lacked.
Life ran, adventurous, focussed
On dogs: a basis unassailable,
Worthwhile, all sun and fun and summer.

So – they married. Zeb knew, I think,
He should not: but it pleased, seeming
To confirm something. Much of Zeb
Married three dogs, and he knew that too.
Well, something forward done, despite
The pain that, seeded, grew.

          I can't make light
Of it at this stage. I do know all
Zeb's done; understood much; well, some
Of it. Now, we are at the point
Where I should have withdrawn,
Left him, deliberately lost touch.
Yet, he has shown some patience
With student ignorance, intractability;
The least that I can do is,
A little longer, suffer his.

Come off it. That's a rationalised excuse.
I should have gone, ceased all hope
For the hopeless, cut the rope.
Yet feel myself, again, dragged on with him;
Knowing that this last outrage ties me in
For ever; makes me of
Him, perpetrator, guilty, punishable
Myself: unrepentant, too. The dogs
Had made me also fall in love.

Thum was black, a tangled mass
Of hair, without defined limits;
Front and back much alike;
Confusing, busy, a bit contrary.
Housewife-like, fussy
With two offspring, twins.

Aery – correctly Aeropagitica –
Small, orange-ginger; short hair, long curvy tail;
A circus dog who should have used
Only rear legs, forever perpendicular. A little scared,
But loving.

Her twin (a larger matter, this):
He looked so much unlike her, as
To be some cosmic jest.
Big, a bit dim,
Mostly white, long-haired,
He looked as if he wore
A loose dog-suit borrowed from
Some chance Old English Sheepdog, but
A size too large.
He had, always, a look of
Mild confusion on his face.
Too funny, far too lovely; he was
A sort of cliché of appeal, endearment,
Who vaguely wished to be a dog,
Or something close. Ben never quite found out.
But Zeb knows: he was
The Essence of Benevolence.

He'd amiably chase
Amanda, the stray cat taken in; she
Who'd coil around your neck, as a fur snake

Or tippet. You'd hear a skelter-roar
As an approaching train.
Amanda passes, stops; here
Comes Ben, all good nature, at
Full speed. Amanda looks, sinks
Down a little; shrinks; watches with interest.
Ben tries to stop, slides
On old polished boards,
Crashes into the wall; shakes
Huge hairy head, confused,
But not more than usual.
Amanda's there, two feet away, still,
Watching. He does nothing, not knowing
Anything to do. He looks embarrassed.
Another Disney moment gone.
All's quiet again.

He had fits; nursed through, survived.
At the break, Zeb's wife took him
Rightly, on grounds of prior ownership.
And so he is absorbed into the past.
Dear aimless simple Ben. ...
It seems to fit:
That sort of innocence
Is not for this world.

Some movement, sudden, and he was there
At sunset, near the house, above the desert scrub.
He paused; gazed: Zeb saw, spoke:
Hello, old lad. Ever so hesitant,
The tail moved, but very little. A perfect
Alsatian: on the small side – a cub,
Not much past puppyhood,
It seemed. He caught the tone,
Meaning, beyond the words; understood;
Came forward; the moment simply, simply good.

How can it be –
A contract setting years of joy,
Adhered to, scrupulously;
Anxiety, exultation, understanding,
Love – be forged so instantly?
Mirror image, complement
To some depth in the self, sent
Free, physically there, granted.

A decade on
And Zeb away, he, my friend, old now, ran off
To the woods, and died; lying quiet,
No mark on him. Zeb, long away,
Was back, next day. Did he not wish
To hurt Zeb with his dying?
Grief-fantasy, that well may be. But it would be
Far beyond fantasy to set out the ways
Of marvel, of the years
Between the two marked days –
Meeting and shrouded parting.
How can you work out, analyse
A piece of souls' creating,
Gone, dead, waiting?

178

Dry desert scrub;
Path, skirting hillock
On the right;
Day, warm to hot, bright
As always.
Four dogs, trotting, jaunty, then –
Then frozen, Pompeii-like,
Stilled in one moment, all askew
As some false tableau (Zebulon too).

It was there. Round a thirst-dead tree;
Just the huge middle, coiled,
Immobile: a contest in waiting.
Fawn, light putty, towards the yellow;
Scales most dimly glazed
Like finger nails, but, darkening,
Forming the great brown diamonds.
Thick, thick – you might have got
Two hands round, stretching thumbs,
If he were well, well dead.
No narrow fellow, occasionally riding,
This one. Nothing moved; an age. He
There. But slowly, so slowly, each scale
Altering, moving to change its light,
He drew, drew round the tree base
All his length (observed now, retrospectively,
As *circa* one-and-a-half Zebulons)
Up the sand-slope, to camouflaged
Light and shade;
Nothing.

It took long.
His head not seen; himself never known,
He was gone, oozed,

Melted to sandy soil, and sun. Dazed,
Four dogs, and Zeb, moved on,
Sobered, awed; assurance gone.
Something lost,
Something contacted, altering the day,
Altering the lives a little
From another age.
Primal. So he lives, the snake,
In this mind, and in the souls
Of four dogs, now long dead.

The Trek: back to the East.
He'd wanted that. California had
Begun to seem a day adrift
From some mind-centre that was real
Still, for Zeb – where vital things, well, ill,
Happened, arriving West as news, just one day late.
He could feel that without defining Real
Or Centre; but its western edge
Ended around Chicago. He had an offer;
Could leave the unthriving academic plant,
California Creeper,
And go.

        The little caravan
Assembled: Zeb, young wife, four dogs now
(One new small Shepherd
Taken in. There he had been, in desert
Near the house; a look lone, doubtful, lost.
Zeb reaches out: he trusts, approaches;
There you are: a birth, a new life
Given in trust: (Chum).
Human freight, too: English
Old school-friend, touring the States;
Having acquired a girl companion,
English, tourist as well. Embroiling. Zeb knew
Its pitfalls – but what could he do?
His old friend lost, a strange new view
Of the familiar: this time, another in the toils, hopeless-
    happy
To be so: worried at complexities
Impending: new sights, new moments
More precious-passing to the friend
Lost, ensnared, condemned.
Zeb empathised: himself half settled-seeming.

181

It's more than possible that he'd grown up
A trifle. And if a moment soured, or warned,
The dogs would make him love, and laugh
It back again. The dogs!

It slowly moved, through heat, and space, the West,
This entourage, in Zeb's old Rambler,
Bought in New Haven, turned towards home again;
The older British Alvis, open tourer,
Maroon and satin-grey,
With its great long shiny nose,
A wheeled Cyrano, needing work, but its past
A *Concours d'Elegance* triumph.
They'd sunk resources for it, in
A grand and careless fling, and as a sign
Of what seemed joy.

They looked, laughed,
Found the cheap motels; climaxing evening meals.
Happy-tired by evening; achieving, free
From roots, doubt, choice. See them all;
Dogs, cars, friends; except the cars, all young;
Astonished in Las Vegas, flat in Reno,
Intrigued in Salt Lake City; there
Zeb forced, from a reluctant bookstore,
A non-Mormon life of Joseph Smith
(No one knows his history).
He, Zeb – not Joseph Smith – swam in
The Great Salt Lake: see Zeb float;
He cannot swim, but does not sink
As usual: flails his arms, swims
Once in his life.

The goldfish, nurtured,
Cherished two thousand miles, is found
In a damp patch on the floor-well; is nursed

182

To health, then dies – it seems
From Chicago water: the only sad event.
See the company, dogs carefully on leash
(Zeb too) walk round Niagara in the sun
And spray.

         Watch them arrive
In triumph, in a cooler East; regretting
Journey's end. Routine awaits.
The house, found through the job,
Is ready: old, lovely, a treasure
Of white boards, green shutters, with land,
A lawn, at bargain rent, from
Sympathetic country-squire. They build
A dog-pen, that seemed
To enclose the past, the odyssey
And, in the persons of the dogs, a winning
From past love, new; shut out
The world; and hold within
Hope. All's new: if late, still a beginning.

Climate in winter: Siberian.
And in a place the size
Of Bradford, there is nowhere, no one
To place stray dogs. So they take them in.

First, collect leashes; sort out
Carefully: five branches on one, four on two others;
Thirteen in all; precisely, one per dog. Zeb
Manoeuvres fourteen sets of feet (counting his own)
To motion. Four dogs ahead; four to right side,
A little behind; five to the left.
Cross the traffic road; walk up the country road
To fields; then follow paths, through woods, to stream.
Let the dogs off; sit thinking by the stream;
Watch water singing over pebbles. Think
Of money, emergencies, plans; hope,
Then worry. So, back to dogs: call,
Whistle; listen; whistle, call.
If there's a rustle, freeze. Relief
As each one comes; if one still
Is missing, wait. Sometimes it's four
Or five. Wait, wait longer; longer; then leave
To pay the waiting-worry-frantic bill,
And hope. Success this time:
One or two late, but here. Adjust the leashes;
Wander home, having achieved.
Go to work.

You learn precisely how it's done
When the time comes: when dread
Becomes this day, this hour; surrounds, poisoning
The air, pressing it down. It's come, as it had to.
But here, now. Go into automatic; be
A machine. The vet comes to the car; Pink
Lies in the blanket, in the boot.

Mind may be anaesthetised,
Yet still move, feel:
As though some mental, quasi-dental
Injection, has not completely
Taken.

You move back, against the will,
Just a trifle, a lifetime:
Sam's daughter, newborn pup
Thought dead (in a shame that cannot,
Will not be told), buried, who made
The earth stir. Zeb ran, tore her up
With his hands. This Phoenix grew
To be Pinky: strange, loving, greedy,
Magic. Short tough gold hair;
Great long legs; half Sam-hound,
Half Setter; a most odd mix, and nervous;
And a sense of humour – one that fits
A second life. A dog that could contrive,
Play jokes, at your expense;
A small thing: thirteen years of joy,
Fun, wonder, love, before calcification
Set in: back legs supported by us,
And a towel, slung underneath
As long as possible, leading
To this moment.

185

You hold her close; are one.
Could she be wishing to die
Just as you? The injection.
It takes place. The mercy is
You cannot tell the moment
Of the going. You wrap her up;
Staggering under the weight, bury
Her in her woods.

It's much the same
With Ted. The big, perfect
Shepherd, with the Husky ruff.
Time's nonsense. You see him through
The window: go out. He leaves
The dry old bone he's found
And wants, as he expects the kick
Or gun. But, in the end convinced, he comes.
He guards us for a decade. Zeb never can
Quite take in his beauty; you don't
Get that in life, and certainly not free.
He's apt to run off, having been free:
Is shot – a buttock full of lead
Cuts out a great muscle.
He's nursed through it: weeks, months.
When infection's at its worst,
You sit in your chair, he
Lying beside, depressed. You need
A pad of cheap perfume to breathe through,
Against the smell of putrifying flesh.
He comes through; for years more
Of miracle. Years of everything.
Then this again.
You hold him, too. The same, again.
The scene, held in terror,
Is here, again.

That moment, when they left,
Slipped into death:
Is it ordered that you shall not know
The instant of the change, rending,
Ravaging? You did not recognise the time
When the entwined self was born.
Why should you know the ending?

Revenants –
The ghosts come again.
Dump, the perfect, simple-silly
Silky Sheepdog, found on a rubbish dump.
We found homes for her puppies; could not place her.
A fussy lady, asking little; nervous,
She with the deep-pool eyes.

Dear Branwell: last survivor,
Who set the date of Zeb's
Retirement, when he died.
How much of life, then, was moulded
By quarantine laws.

When Zeb
Was quite alone, except for dogs,
He heard a scuffle-noise one winter night
At the front door. Thrown over the fence
From passing car, it was Bran:
Tiny, indeterminate pup, with
The huge feet, that wrapped
Around Zeb's neck like clock-weights
Upon strings. He should become
The large Alsatian type, Zeb thought,
He, with those feet. He never did.

As lone survivor,
He seemed to inherit, embody
And pass on all love lost
Into the present. When he died –
Wife coping, suffering that –
Zeb away, it was the end.

New life, old country; home next,
Dogless, with the heart split.
Last, lost.

To speak of love's embarrassing;
Of dogs, to most, a bore.
Zeb knows he's done too much
Of both; will speak of one dog more.

One who contains it all:
Who was immune, bigger than
Pain, or tragedy, or death.
This one was above it all;
This one had life solved;
Imposed himself on it;
Still makes character, defiant;
Still teaches Zeb. This one,
King of Insouciance,
Was conqueror.
He shall have words
To testify
What he was;
Have them as gift;
His own.

Zeb met him in the village, in
Worst winter's outrage:
Twenty below, snow, ice everywhere;
A slicing wind cutting temps.
To Unspeakable. He could well
Have been enjoying a midsummer trot.
Zeb spoke: he came up, stood;
Substantial, not huge; muscles,
Muscles like iron bands, protruding.
An Atlas dog: broad, near-mastiff
Head; essence of mongrel: dark brown-
Ginger hair, coarse, short, stiff. He stood,
Allowed a few pats

190

(As a concession only); chat
Ended (he decided), he trots
Into the swirling freeze.

It happened six or seven times
Within three bitter weeks. He strayed
Into Zeb's head, haunting.
No use resisting more; Zeb asked,
Begged him. In the end,
As favour granted, he stayed.
Sam. Samson-Muscles.
Sam-Never-Give-a-Damn.

He made a friend of Chum.
Tolerated the others, also us;
Kept himself to himself – except that once
When he got out, to visit Krismus,
The Irish Setter, carefully separated, on heat;
Sam fathering Pinky and others, then
Retired to his pen.

                    You could tell
He thought a lot of you, even
Felt a bit. For when you stroked
Or patted him, even embraced,
He'd take on a thoughtful look;
Great broad brow puckering
In the frown, above the eyes,
As if he were considering
Ways to return affection, wished
But not yet quite worked out.

He must go to the vet – some growth,
Worrying, on his head. He took no notice
Of the whole thing: sat in the open car,
His first ride; faced backward, considering

191

The past, with an occasional frown. Motorists
At stop lights, pointed, laughed a bit,
Waved, before he quelled them with a glance
That never saw them. He ignored
The vet, the needle; travelled back with the same
Regal distance; never changed.

You learn from dogs, and that's no slick inversion.
When Zeb is most himself, lost, uncertain,
Facing a future this or that,
Intimidated; there comes a leading, a coercion:
A little piece of Sam (memory seeming fired
By chance) touches the mind. Zeb does
The gutsier thing, not natural
To him; given, gratefully acquired.

In the end,
Zeb away, he was set upon
By the pack of dogs. He fought
Until the wounds were mortal;
Then travelled, undistressed,
More himself than ever
For the *coup de grace*,
Which he could take
Or leave. Zeb had five years
With Sam, before that day. I think Death
Must have been shaken, quite a bit
When Sam ambled in.

I

A last sea voyage, on the *France*;
Much like others, though ship and food
Are fine. This is the great, planned
Sabbatical journey. Zeb feels secure
Professionally; the Karmann Ghia
Sports convertible, black, is delivered
Only two days late, at Southampton docks:
The only new car Zeb
Has ever owned, or will own.

May was the start. With young wife
To Holland (great volcanic quarrel,
Possessive, smouldering into Germany before
Eruption, over some indefinite night foray).
O Zeb! Zeb!

           Germany, all swift
Autobahn: Austria (the tapestry
Long searched for, found at Klagenfurt).
Jugoslavia, with border war memorials
Of atrocities in mute green places
Set among hills: hills, plains, woods;
Roughnesses, suspicions, lorries, truck-stops
All gathered in by the great road south.
Skopje, resting after earthquake; Belgrade,
A large hotel suite, cheap, in dull-dead city.
Greece is the sweep of waterfront at
Salonika, the hills behind. Then, the little
Virgin beaches, bare, private, still;
The distant shadow of Olympus;
The waterfall with ghosts, at Larissa;
The whispering locked calm at Delphi.
Athens, where reality meets expectation,

Yet set in dusty chaos. Istanbul, almost
Small then: mosques, narrow mysteries, bridge;
Soccer one Sunday by the walls; near
Topkapi's Arabian Nights; the bent
Shrouded women working fields, who stared,
Waved, towards Ankara. Friends there,
And the intimate relics
Of Atatürk. Then Piraeus,
Bari, Rome, to rendezvous with family
At Venice, after six weeks
Of panorama show, which age
Will alter to panopticon.

                One memory
Encapsulating all, remaining?
Zeb knew one word of modern Greek: *Poi*,
Meaning, "Well. ..." And passing through
Some primal broken village in North Greece,
One hairy ragged peasant sees
The shiny black sports car,
Long hair of the blonde, streaming
In wind: words trailing into space,
Shouts with a Falstaff zest and lust, "O
Poi, poi, poi, poi-oi-oi-oi ..."
His meaning a perfection
Of international clarity.

Change
Was not obvious;
Not much to do with Zeb's wonder-lust
Or lusts; or the exquisite illogic
Of marriage laws. It was substantially,
Almost entirely,
A matter
Of courtesy.

It could, it should, have had
Causes more standard, acceptable:
Her long longing for a child
(Until that was fulfilled); his unrest, drive,
Drive towards polygamy; that
Unfulfilled. The love for dogs,
Shared, could have overridden those
With ease. No. It was this other thing,
Absurd on the face of it,
Too powerful in the end.

He had to have the courtesies;
Made miserable by their lack;
Needed the daily signs
Of reassurance. English, English enough.
She, younger, required a brashness
As mask for her uncertainties;
Took joy in breaking rules,
Conventions; flouting politenesses.
American, she who,
With one single, simple Fuck You,
Could inflict long isolating wretchedness,
Sudden, more penetrating,
Than a blow. Two modes

Of coping, never coming near;
Never to cohere.

She left; took child, her dogs,
Dear Amanda, the cat; leaving
Him his dogs; commitments
Never discussed, but clearly known.
The rest, soap opera:
He harassed by her shyster
Lawyer, until he turned, enraged.
What miracle of energy, zest,
Is liberated, when lovers, become best
Friends, are sudden formal enemies!
He settled into work and dog-routine:
Drive to work; back at mid-day
To walk the dogs;
Back to work; home; fifty-two
Miles a day; evening walk; evenings
Blessed; telephone tamed;
Alone with dogs. The puppy,
Branwell, is, one winter night,
Thrown on the front step: a help.
Zeb, sent some sales list, finds The Book
Owned, once, by the second Charles; sends for it
With all his cash – one great defiant blow,
Thinking, hold on; when Branwell came, something
Must improve.

Last glimpse. One noon, in the village's
Post Office, he glanced across the road;
Saw her, outside her new apartment
Hanging clothes; the tiny figure
Of their daughter, just having learned
To stand, watching, among the dogs lost.
The urge to rush across almost
Propelled him there. He fought, resisted,
Left. The few feet between, in time
Became three thousand miles.
It could as well have been
Ten, two, or infinity. That was all.

This woman has been his Friend
A quarter-century; asks nothing;
Understands; leans in Zeb's favour.

She has Beauty,
The very thing itself, that words gather to
Like filings on a magnet.
For her, crowds would shift,
Ill at ease, only half resentful, awed.
I heard a woman say, without malice,
But a half-anger, "How can we compete
With that?"

Have you,
As Zeb has, watched Beauty,
Glimpsed over years, unaltering;
Longing, destructively, for it to dim,
Pass, sink to the everyday, take
Temptation, envy, away under its arm,
Should usage and convention, barriers,
Break?

It became possible
To talk, alone – a dinner
At some London place
Or other. Zeb, back to wall,
Speaks all his burden, hopes;
Watching this glowing thing,
All harmony, all energy with peace,
Certainty, goddess, haven
Three feet away, near him; near his.
Hours are obliterated, made extinct.

198

He saw a diner goggling,
Hypnotised, shameless, entranced;
Studied the man held staring by
A miracle – not simply her, but
The mix of them both, gilded, an elevation.
Years on, he wonders still
What the man saw, that
He will not forget. Zeb himself
Saw only lifelight, felt
Only the upward surge
Of joy, wonder-joy, singing, soaring
Up, from loins, to stomach, heart,
Head, brain, life;
He being inside, as some integral
Part of it.

NINETEEN SEVENTIES

She is leaving
A moribund life, and by choice.
From the respectable, routine
To minor scandal runs:
Outrage, family alienation
As former friends give voice,
The righteous ones.

Climax: flight. Zeb drives
The car towards escape.
Pauses, confused, afraid, half-
Way, by abbey ruins set in green;
Walks a summer lane; this is
The last of choice: finality, crisis.
Turn back, East, to the past;
Go on, West, to future. Never
One, Zeb, to reject the faintly
Possible, despite experience. Unsaintly,
Never turned his back on hope,
However slim. So they flew,
On the day arranged,
Together.

Do you see
Loveliness, dignity, pressed low
Towards a car floor, avoiding tongues,
Anger, at spy-points in the leaving?
And all for what? For Zeb.
Let's hope he knows, might even
Learn, once, from this right deceiving.

They drive
To Scottish places, for ten days
Inviolate. This mature two, in

Late forties, bound in love,
Pride in each other: they cannot bear
To be adult. Back, then, to face
The necessary music: separately;
He to America, she visa-waiting.
Months on, she comes, Zeb's friends celebrating.
She makes order, winds bonds
Of love-routine about the dogs.
Other months pass: happy, work-happy.
When it can be, they marry, guestless,
Private, in Montrose, Pa., the small
White wooden town all set in green.
Save your breath, and mine.
We need not fear for Zeb, this time.
He is unworried. There is a gravity,
A way ahead, this time. The ceremony
Unnecessary.

                 The first advertisement
They look at, hopelessly, finds
A small knocked-about house
In country hills; it costs
Seven thousand dollars. Lawns,
Two acres of woods, below a rolling heath
Of spaces, trees, and bush; perfect for dogs.
They make the house firm, and their own.
Build a dog-pen, dog-bedroom (ten
Square feet) just off the little library.
She, in the days, works, decorates,
And tries to place two thousand homeless dogs.

Is this the perfect end – even, for Zeb?
O, it rocks, will rock, at times.
What thing, moment, event,
Suggests the strength of it?
I think it must have been

When they moved to their shabby,
Doubtful, new old house. The truck
Hired, packed with their everything:
Dogs, books, bits, furniture,
Mirrors. She is inside, calming the dogs.
The great door slams, echoes. Zeb drives
The sixteen miles, badly, worried, haltingly:
Is there ventilation? What is
This quiet, to the rear? The stop-lights last
For ever; he stops; goes to the back
At half-journey; calls through the door
At sliding, scrambling, barking, whining:
A desperate, taut answer: – Go on; don't
Open that door. There, in there,
Is his everything; his Helen
With Zeb's life, and lives,
In this steel Trojan horse.

           All is accomplished, well.
That evening they have day's only meal
In a small bar. They eat,
Drink; look, and look; feel
Exultation, relief, anticipation, all
With the exhaustion, making full happiness.
She did all this, and for Zeb.
The wonder's that. Believe, believe
In that one wonder, for it survives
Assaults, deaths, another country,
Another quarter-century, and
Goes on, lives.

University Quintet

I

104 *Meaningful Dialogue*

He came upon a crowd
In the quadrangle;
Above, on the raised walkway,
A platform, rigged for emergencies.
Up there, the University President, one
Pleasant, conforming to all trends, so very
Adaptable, modern, ready; made
Of good quality wax, that means
No harm: all reasonable, formal,
Neat, well-dressed: there, with him, in the sun,
Two or three students – leaders,
The crowd said – all in uniform; which means
Beads, beards, hair (stubble and long)
And jeans.

It was Zeb's first view
Of Meaningful Dialogue: nothing plain said;
Subject not defined, or indicated.
He saw the student seize
The harmless amiable figurehead
By his symbolic part, the tie
(The only tie in seven hundred peers),
And shake him by the throat
To rising cheers.

Released, frightened,
The man swallowed, looked grateful, spoke
Gently, reasonably, at some
Length, saying nothing. Zeb, altered,
Passed on to teach his class,
Knowing, some new

And crucial evil born;
Day changed from sun,
Soul sinking, knowing
An old world going, war begun.
A world gone leaves its remnant, its unwanted part
New undesired commitment, loth.
Unwilled, fixed now: this, this is to fight –
The fated grasp of oath
Upon the heart.

He just avoids being small.
Dapper-handsome, controlled, relaxed;
Benevolent look: a fairly eminent
Doctor, you might guess now;
Just faintly veering towards
Some oddly benign businessman, yet
All alert intelligence, intellect, brow.

Made in America, arrived
From Italy when he was four;
Good Catholic, of course; strict family;
Bookish, carving his way to Harvard, Brown.
Then a respected Chairman of Humanities.
A telling naïveté there, Chairman, administrator
With a medieval troth
For living the believing:
Humane principles; simple decencies;
Both.

When Ignorance and Energy
Meet with Illusion, fall in love
(One of those wry tricks
Of timing), then reading,
Thinking, shrink to politics,
Fall into step in the rebellion-shove,
It will take more than afraid,
Part-educated cliques to turn back
That parade.

Nonetheless, the Believing Man, and Zeb, made
Just such a group: thirty professors. It spread
To groups across the state; achieved no more
Than showing such a thing as head

Remained; could tell some bodies not to march.
It bequeathed, besides, an analysis
(Using five hundred dummy souls) of academe.
Twenty per cent fell into student step,
Most cling-sycophants, up-
To-the-minute Trendies; a few
Small would-be Lenins. About
Six per cent joined with resistance; gave
With names and cash (a few
Cash only, privately). The rest, the large
Majority, sat on a wide and comfortable
Fence, one nicely curved for the behind,
Where courage hid; they waited
To see which way to lean
In some uncertain future time; then only
Cautiously, no more than just a bit,
Till the entire matter be debated.

Zeb worked some years,
Wrote here and there
Against the trends. It's odd,
Sudden, to be employed
By university, revelling
In rebellion, making a void
Where the books were: colleges now
Machines for social levelling.

Is your average human
Worth more than that? Zeb came
To doubt it: ended his active service
To retire. He felt some shame
To trust in pendulum swings;
Turning away; leaving time
That changes all, to regain
Real things.

Not so, for the Believing Man:
Retired also, now, thirty years on;
Health doubtful, going or gone.
He still lives near the university,
The ever-unwelcome *J'Accuse*;
Active, industrious, still
The scholar, but knowing how
To make outrage, absurdity
Known, where it counts;
Awakening parents, public
Just a little, now.

Zeb, back turned (and in another land
Almost as sick, the copy-way)
Is wiser, with a wisdom tainted.
The better man, Believing,
He who cannot choose
To cease his war, or bend;
Beyond defeats, decade by decade
To his life's end,
He cannot lose.

106 Degree Award

They meet, eight qualified men,
To mark exams, for the degree,
Master of Arts. (Exam essays
Identified by numbers only,
For objectivity.)

All papers read; values agreed.
All that remains
Is to put name to screed.
Here's a unanimous
Failing, that shows a lack
Of everything. Catastrophe!
She's black.

A nice person, Chairman says;
Who's worked hard, adds another.
A mature person, says a third: and a mother.
Chairman, a man of standards, firm,
Fair, does a sudden schizophrenic turn;
Suggests a pass. Zeb protests, passionately.
There's no debate. It passes;
Seven to one, and so does she.

She takes her new M.A.
Back to the deep South.
New qualified, by mouth-
Assent, for her new station:
The liberal advancement
Of black education.

Zeb never thought
To see his failed
Student again.
He had explained
Why she had failed
Two years ago.
She's come to say
She'd got a B+, now,
From Mr. So-and-So.

Zeb went again
Through reasons why
She'd failed his course;
Suggesting, though,
She must be better
Two years on. She could go
Equally, to enquire why
She'd done so well, now,
For Mr. So-and-So.

She did just that:
Wept, wept, when she came back.
"Why was my grade so good?"
She'd asked.
He'd said,
"Because you're black."

Zeb looks back
On the struggle years.
Was it worthwhile?
He never knew
Until, the other day,
When, on TV
He
Heard Shirley Williams say,
Quite angrily,

"In the 'seventies,
There was ...
Consensus
On comprehensives,
Which broke
Because of the
So-called
Black Papers
Authors."

And, Sir, be it noted
That I (and Zeb)
Do both aver
That praise
Is accurately quoted.

Zeb had to smile.
It was worthwhile.

Sohrab and Rustum gone,
At least the Oxus floated on
In struggle, yet a kind of peace.
Below the stars, the river wends;
Some faint romantic hope, some spark
After the bright high birth in Pamere;
Still beauty dimly luminous in the dark
(The poem is much an exercise in light).
Some hope, then, to reach some ends?
That there could be
A possibility;
Some form, some goal –
The Aral Sea.

But now, the news tells me, this Grail, the top
Of possibility,
Is now a sacrificial sop
To scientific productivity,
And loss of credibility.
There is no star to shine
In hope of possibility,
Upon the Aral Sea,
Which has dried up.

Inside the hall, the noise and talk of men;
The fire, the minstrel's chant, the amber glow
Of mead: outside, the moan of wind, the ice, the swirling
    snow.
A sudden flutter in the air, and then
A flash of feathers circling the hall,
Above the ruddy warmth, the sweat, the song.

Touching between the beams, along
The chilling sodden stones, and to the wall
And out into the blank and bitter cold.

This bird glimpsed life itself: no less, no more; a night
Of vague and thoughtless shadow; then the dazzling birth
Into the maze of colour, shape and light,
And out again; out to the null and senseless grip of earth.

We also know no more: it would be well to learn
Of some new teaching.

*(Based on a vignette in the Anglo-Saxon version of Bede's
  Ecclesiastical History – Paulinus and Edwin.)

They had been friends
In the Raf.
He hardly ever wrote: a most lax
Correspondent. Then a sudden,
Joyous letter sends
The facts.

Two rugby lads, close friends,
Anxious, once Saturday's game ends
To get out on the pee,
And early: "Come home with me,"
Says Host. "Have your shower
At my house, and we're away;
We'll save at least an hour."

Guest, as seems fit, showers first; soaps
Hair; next, rinsed, sings amid the steam;
Stands towelling his head, that muses evening hopes.
Door opens; enter wife of Host. It seems
Most odd. She ambles easily through the mist;
Places, deliberately, on window ledge,
A cup of tea; walks back to doorway's edge,
Where a Thought strikes, and persists.
She moves back to the turbaned monument,
Doubt-stilled, freeze-framed,
Who has not reacted;
And firmly flicks his steam-contracted
Dangling part; without the least intention to cause pain,
But with affection, and a precise aim
Of manicured, conservatively-tinted nail
Of middle finger.

        She sets sail;
He still a rock; amazed –

216

Especially at her *au revoir* –
"Tea up, Cock!"
Follow her, wondering, down
To her kitchen. She makes
Herself some tea. Raising cup
To lips, her gaze moves idly up
Through curtains, window; takes
In the familiar garden path, the gate,
Which clicks; she sees, as on some ghastly stage,
The lower portions of her legal mate
Approach, beneath the *Green Sports* page.

I fear I can't record or reckon
Her steps of thought
The next few seconds.
Stick to external things:
Husband, diverted from the football scores
By passing, flying spouse;
Wordless, like crossing trains;
She to her mother's house;
Once there, immovable; staying away
Till well into the morning
Of Monday.

NINETEEN EIGHTIES

They look, slightly askance,
Eyes forcing distance, holding back
If they think you write, especially verse;
Thinking their *me* at risk
Or worse.

No need to fret, be smitten.
They live, hurt, happy, brisk,
Against what is true in lives.
And if I write of them
In focus, or in passing,
It is true;
Or it would not be written.

The atoms move, propelled
By forces, ignorant, into the patterns; silk strands hold.
The Papers (Fettercairn) discovered.
Small war ensues; interrupted by
The large one, political, called World War
Two. That done, small Boswell war, covert,
Goes on. The discoverer is Zeb's old Prof.,
Then in his closet, as all such were closeted
Then.

Zeb, now at Yale, plays squash
With Friend. You play squash at Yale
In a cathedral. You can play doubles squash, quite rare,
In a great long field of a chamber;
Zeb and Friend make a decent pair.

Prof., breathing resentments, comes to Yale
Where the Papers are, after the wars, after the sale.
Prof. is ill; has his operation. Zeb and then wife
Look after him; drive him to Harvard, towards
   recuperation.
To hear him talk, he thinks they save his life.
Zeb listens to resentments, takes it in;
Puts nothing out: plays squash with Friend,
Who, in the Boswell factory, deciphered, read;
Edited on. Twenty years, more, pass;
Zeb a continent away. Prof. long dead.

A quarter century strange,
Zeb and old Friend meet in New York;
Have dinner; talk and books exchanged.
Friend long decloseted, mourning
A lover. Zeb is not sure what
Has made him write, suggesting

222

Meeting; simple memory-affection
It seems. He's glad of it. Friend,
Who's had one heart attack,
Dies, soon after.

The web
Is laid out, nicely arranged,
Now. Books sit on shelves, not
Communicating much of their own making, own
History. Old papers, resentments, disputes, law,
Male love, health, disease, death, cash, wars and cases
    won,
And scholarship – all together in the pot
With suitable covers, jackets on.

What would Boswell
Have made of it? Not much, not in the time
He'd wish to give it. A passing
Comment, part pithy, partly crude, about it all.
A bottle, evening odyssey, unarmed, with willing girl,
Against a churchyard wall.

Lone travelling done,
Zeb's back; to find, with another summer,
The dear last dog is gone.
Here, now, new emptiness.

Next day the letter comes, to set out
An early-retirement bribe.
All conspires, fraught
To nudge the change.
The book is out, that seeds
The salary raise, that feeds
The pension, helping it on.
Personnel wars, enmities, plots are fought,
And, this one time, won.

The She-pain is no less, but could be other
In future: less, or more, in another
Country. Wait to see. Even
The establishment warms;
Assumes a front humanity, keeps forms;
Shake hands, all's over, done.
Nothing personal, now,
In this welcome riddance
To an awkward one.

Let the routine presentation
Be stillborn; no formal dinner
To celebrate hypocrisy.
Remain your own.
Go, and quietly.
When change and time loom huge,
It is a kindly mystery
That forces, making disparate things

Combine, singing
To harmony; cohere, smooth endings;
Conceive beginnings.

What is this change?
Is it that they have bulldozed the Pavilion Hotel
Where a Laughton ruled, resembling his brother,
Henry the Eighth?
And lost the Floral Hall of glass
To place brown plastic slabs, instead?
Lord Leighton's house is Woolworth's now,
    rectangular,
And such as he could not have dreamed to paint.
Is it just that old beauty, like a red rag
To a council, has been killed
So all may look the same,
Like the young strangers in the streets?

Is it that Zebulon, come back, is changed
As all things pass?

Rowntrees had carpets every inch
And the smell of luxury.
And the old café had fires
In the tile and iron alcoves;
Waitresses in black and frills,
And muffins in the winter
(Now called English muffins, as in the USA, convenient
For freezing).
And, in the heat,
The balcony that looked upon the street
Across from the old Balmoral Hotel, also
Gone (now Tesco's – or is it parking?)
Which looked down towards the older Bar
That even Zebulon could not know well
Except in paintings, though he knew
The old grocery of the coffee-smell
Where change hummed on the wires.

226

Why are the streets full of ugly people,
The little poor shops blazoned with sales
Announced, mis-spelled, by splotch-posters?
Why does Zeb run away, a fugitive,
Where once he came as lover?

Can half one century
Perform such battery?
Or is it he, dimly remembering
Some illusory will-within
Towards order, peace, harmony?
All the same, then, it was there;
A something: clear, pervasive
In the blue, sun-struck day
That a war cleared away; some Thing
Beyond all possibility of change,
Behind the visible air.

Let me say what I won in the war.

To stand, pressed closely to this girl
(Slim, dark, indeterminate,
Especially in the gloom, slight-looking, gentle
Among the debris of the bombed-out church
Close to the heart of the late empire,
Very near Eros).

I had seen it in the day: jagged blocks,
Broken concrete, stone; rubble piled, with ferns,
Fresh green weeds, rosebay here and there
Poking out of the mess.
"D'you just want me to play about like this, Luv,
Or the real thing?"

Now, decades gone, are there, at moments,
Two shadows, coiled as one,
As the organ swells in the tasteful
Restored church (some fine glass),
(Surely a trick of the half-light)?

O love, where are you now?
Do those generous, gentle, pleasure-probing fingers,
So willing, ten-shilling fingers
Creak slightly at the knuckle-joints
As these do, as I move the pen?

It is, first, decreed:
You must want them all,
But can't succeed.

Yet there need be no trouble,
No questing for years;
But numbers immense,
Lovers various, varied to the infinite
Power. And what you do
Depends on you,
In desire, inventively,
With time, no more destructive:
The wanted moment frozen, still
As art is –
Not TV, ephemerally.
No change,
No talk, approach, persuasion
Nervously.
No persons, pairings, pains, or partings,
But privacy.
No fees, no money risk,
Blackmail, marriage, nor no marriage-crib
With bedposts shifting constantly
By change of law,
At the behest
Of women's lib.,
And other forces, modishly.
No worry, all infection-free;
No Aids, nor Herpes
Nor V.D.
Moreover, soundly philosophic:
For the second decree
Is that thou shalt be, art, alone;

229

As Arnold said, and it must be.
The only reasonable love
Is auto-erotic.

In the middle of my garden
Grows an oak;
Still young, yet tall.
When house and garden go,
It shall be there still
Lording it over the ruins.
Then, when the unknown comes,
Then it shall fall.
The tree of life,
It too shall then fall.
And that is all.

These bones, that make this skeleton,
Since they fell from the womb,
Have shifted seven million times
In travel towards the tomb.

Each move could be computed
Then plotted in advance;
A representational record
Of a primal, ordained dance.

There are one million movements left
To place upon the chart.
These bones have yet to dance with yours
As wished for by the heart.

The arrival by steps, taken in
With surprise: good face; long straight hair
(Always his weakness); coming late,
Skin red-glow from the ice outside;
Beauty: not rare beauty;
But the great big lovely girl
All life-full, overflowing
Slightly, too clumsy for the statuesque;
Great slow Yeatsian thighs
To be lost between. Face
Inviting, to devour a camera's eye;
And placed against dead backdrop
Of committee, with the most festering
Of colleagues, who knew her.
She new, new to Zeb;
He lost in lust and love.

Then months, years, of talk;
Of circumstantial invitation, half-warmth.
Talk: of missing at partings;
Then, only at parting out of danger,
The lone, lorn embrace.
Moments frozen in warmth: the brain retains
The face, years, years after.
The white coat modelled for approval
In mother's presence, even
As if Zeb were legitimate and free,
A member of the family.

Fidelity, growing wasteful
Increasingly: the rushes, over time
Of longing-sickness, sickness, lost:
Chains kept after parting
In another country.

Chains can grow, like ivy.

Then, linked years after,
The revelation:
Kept (as ever, but now more clear) at distance,
Half pushed away, nervously
And half-invited: a return
To familiar chains;
Treated ill now, slave-like.
Then, away again. Reflecting on that,
Surprisingly
A little free.
And God, in thy mercy,
Made her seem
Grown fat as well;
And he was free,
He thought,
In most ways free.
Well, substantially.

Five Cities

I

121   London

The boy was fifteen; stayed with his aunt
Who kept the shop. He'd never seen
Such massive green
As Nonesuch Park, near Cheam.
Once, allowed into the city
As evening fell, a woman, lovely,
Took his breath from him. Motherly;
Called him so softly from a shop doorway
In Piccadilly. She must have been
Twenty-five at least; dark; so much
The lady, nestled in white furs.
Beauty and terror, mixing, propelling
As explosives in a gun, shot him away,
A matter of regret for fifty years.

He was there in the war
From time to time; expectation
Fought confusion, and confusion won.
There was a V-Day: out, and reeling
With his oppo, and by ten a.m.,
Just off Trafalgar Square. Uniforms
Seemed not to help, but who
Can be sure, as the day dissolved
In memory-mist, even as it unrolled?

Then years of visits, passings through, flickers
Of memory. Blankers-Koen in orange knickers;
Gailly, staggering his rending yards
Of Marathon-lap, and overtaken
Twice. Shops, with bargain luxuries;
Good pencil sketches; one or two loving looks;

Busts, and old maps, and books.
We now have democratic levelling,
And all have rights, from Cardboard
City to the Savoy (which are quite close).
But then, you could go to
The Corner House, Coventry Street,
And be a little lord for twelve and six,
Including wine. Zeb's often wondered
Why you could never get
A table free at Fortnum's just for tea,
It being ever crammed and touristy;
When down below, in Simpson's, tea
Was spacious, grave, peaceful, gentle-
Manly. Theatres, cheap, could strike
You like a thunderclap, and new, new, new.
When Zeb would come, it was the start
Of summer: Lord's, with the new touring team;
A bit on the chill side, but a beginning
Promise-filled. Even the dancing
Stripping girls in Soho seemed warm,
Friendly: the rackets not yet hardening.
You could pack the day: shops, V & A,
The War Museum, pubs, the dancing girls,
Tea, theatre, all swiftly won, by tube.
Pleasure looked back, whipping the hours
To frenzy. From ruins grew weeds and flowers.

Do not forget
The blonde girl from South Africa,
With the white boots, who spoke
To Zeb on the bus. They had the day
To spare, and night before her flight; drinks
In the Market pub; sights, a wonder-luck
Felt, and by both. Zeb had to see war-
Friends, at a reunion. A bit surprised,
He kept that meeting, missing the set

Night. O Zeb, are you growing, acquiring late
Standards? Regret, regret!

In the club: Zeb, with his friend,
And friend's wife; the Spanish waiter,
Also a dancer, with the heels and castanets
(But not a dancing-waiter), ignored totally
Friend's wife, and glided off to fetch Zeb's coat
On leaving; helped him on with it; pinched two
  folds
Of his cheek: "You, you're far too nice,
To catch cold."

There was Eve, who did not like to wait.
But nights brought sleepless energy in flood.
The miles, limitless, walking, walking,
Driven, seeking; courage-conversation;
Lust that stops short, bitten by hope
Of different, kinder, more, invention,
Violence, newness. O, the miles, and hours
To three and four and five, then morning light;
Exhaustion in pursuit of more, and smiles
As entrance to it. Girls in the Park
Who climbed the railings. The blonde
With long trailing hair, in Shepherd Market,
Who exclaimed, "What a marvellous prick!"
At an unveiling.

                    Odd that the walking,
Endless, should have ended
In love-walk: the thing itself;
Two walking, walking the city,
Because they cannot bear to part.
This new thing born: they end
Holding tea mugs with the porters
In Covent Garden – knowing, crying,
Something born is something going;

Like the Garden, condemned, dying.

That change joined all the rest:
The deadly, dull, depressing, hypocritical
Street Offences Act, that brought the air
Of *Nineteen Eighty Four*. The stroll up Burlington
Arcade; for the magic, quality; worth
The expense. Steadily, it now becomes
Parade of things unwanted but extortionate.
Where is the change – in person, place or both?
Theatres plough on, invention lost;
Compensate with tired revivals at huge cost.

Come back now, to view the site at least.
'Plane lands at dawn. By seven on a Sunday
You stand by King's Cross; no trains
For some two hours. All's grey:
Rubbish of last night blows, flaps up
Against walls, over the drains.
Hotels are one hundred pounds, doubtful;
Two hundred, good. You see
In today's Sunday paper that the thing
For gentlemen (What a prick poses
For the photo!) is an indeterminate
Fishing jacket, dun-dull smock, made
Of sound materials, for seven hundred
And fifty pounds. But just the thing.

Walk down the street, past the sex
Shops. Take care, when you shall sniff
The frying fat of hamburgers; do not slip
On wrappings, cartons (styrofoam) thrown
On the paving stones.

On Zeb's last trip
To town, he came upon a riot: cars burned

Out. Newly informed, he learned
It expressed unrest at the conception
That everyone should pay at least a bit
For local services. Even rebellions, here,
Are shabby ones. He asked a newspaper
Seller for direction to a street nearby.
"Buy a paper," snarled the man, fat, ugly,
"Or get out."

Viewed from away, or on TV
It is the echoing city-house of politics.
You can, however, get to the Continent,
Finding a port, taking a boat
To Rotterdam. Our own city
Can be avoided. If you must go
By flying, stay in the countryside; taxi to Heathrow.
It's well worth the expense
For what you will not see.

The style, joy, spirits are gone.
A city, of some loves,
Has slipped away: buildings left
To obscure. And cars; some
Clamped, some free in traffic jams.
Those, who can't commute half-lives away,
Harassed, racketed, calculating, scared, defeated;
Marks of weakness, marks of woe repeated.
There are still the green places.
The green reproves.

Paris

Some thing is in this air, and changeless.
You grow old: it is the same.
Merely romantic myth of centuries? Rather
A heightening, an extra life
To fantasy. What's possible to dream
Is here, that definition
Would kill. Definition, thank God,
Is not possible.

        Zeb breathed
This air, new to him, and danced
In the streets, Bastille Day, 'forty eight.
All a bit drunk, drunk on air,
Love, being alive, young; till that was killed
By his English friend's turning it
To sex and acquisition. Learn.
It is a teacher. Take
Zeb's phase of out-of-the-question
Desires: there, passing in the street
Is a Doppelgänger: a young, fair
Pretty girl; a mutual stopping,
Magnetic: few words, and at ease; a hotel room,
Clean; a natural joining, straight-
Forward, straight, hugely enjoyed
By both. Words, pleasant, courteous,
Gratitude, bordering affection, and all done
In half an hour.

Take the train to Versailles.
The tingle of anticipation in the stomach
Gilds the journey. Walk the long street.
Buy a cake, eat as you walk, happy.
There it is, the broad open square;

The magic beyond the railings,
Beyond the restored past, the size,
Symmetry; the white and gold
Set in the green, the water-green.
Walk the green distances to their extremes,
To the follies, and if alone,
Catch, in the air beyond the green,
The smallest rustle-hinting from the past,
Just alive, growing, not
Attainable. This is not
The *Adventure* of two English ladies;
Not the history, or the stones,
But stimulus, an alive frisson
Through senseless air, altering
Imagination, to a half half-glimpse
That grips moments, sets up fears.

       Come back to here
And now. The small broken hotel
On Avenue Clichy. All heavy, ancient
In decline part-arrested, pausing:
The great bed; things cracked or broken;
Costs tiny, even with a balcony, over the street,
Where you stand to try
To believe. Go to the one appalling
Toilet, that serves all rooms: it is
Soon over, with your dread, then half-shame
That you could avoid it, buying better.
Forgive; this place is Paris. Return
To this hotel over the years; even bring
One you love here. She acquiesces
In your love of the place: another
Joining, and firm.

       Before, being Zeb,
Be driven, always driven. Look, look again

241

In the *patisserie* next door, and see
A woman, mature, lovely; French-ripe, haunting.
Gaze, gaze on, suffer, through the window.
Driven, driven, prepare your French,
Force body to automaton, and ask.
Defy each speck of your withdrawing mind.
The warmth of the refusal, kind,
Pleased, makes the ordeal worthwhile.
Be glad you saw.

Walk, walk.
Fall to your city-scouring, driven,
Possessed by ghosts sought: the trek
Is like a home, familiar, all at one.
Drink in a bar. Walk, walk
(You cannot do it now)
The *Boulevard des Italiens*.
Sit at a pavement table; watch, walk, walk
Into the small hours: cherish
Moments of hope, half-finding;
And of escape.

Begin with a meal
In a small place on Montmartre
Hill: simple, good, cheap.
Or the Polish place, a bit ambitious,
Respectful, sound. Resume the walk;
Probing, searching.

Go to Lachaise: see the guard
Leap toy-like from his box, to gather alms.
Observe his monumental hopeless shrug,
As you slip with the currency,
Giving a trifle. The hideous
Tomb of Oscar is further
Defaced, by some 'sixties tag; no one

Here, now, to turn that into wit.

Finding.
One summer Sunday evening, on the Rivoli,
Zeb looked into a window, expensive
Of course: *Louvre des Antiquaires*.
He is lost, transfixed. The gilded
Bronze statuette, Colleoni of Verrocchio
Strikes his eyes, his mind, a stagger-blow.
Zeb swallows, dizzy, lost; he's seen
The source in Venice; never this. He is in love,
Possessed, troubled to frenzy. How long
Has he gazed, stupefied? When did he
Break off, resume his walk, pace redoubled, in a trance?
He is unnoticing of women, people, Paris.
He cannot sleep, being haunted, calculating.
Somehow he communicates, 'phones, raises
Cash here and there, takes all he has,
And buys it somehow; arranges
That it be sent, export permitted, to England;
Breaks off his stay; leaves penniless,
Returns to America, still
In love, with hope, joy, future
Uncontained. Months go: battles
With British red-tape: the war is bloody,
Tape deep red, gory. Zeb wins;
Authority, worn, surrenders. The French Horse
Unpacked after a year, is beautiful, as in first shock;
Zeb still in love, and deeply,
With a thing, an object, and the everything
It always brings; will bring.

Prague, 1975

July, in England. From America, the wire arrives.
Jan, dear Czech friend, had tried annually
And for years, for the visa permitting him to see
Again, his city. Now, at last he has it.
Come, said the cable: I'll show
You Prague. Zeb and wife promptly packed
And went. The ship from Hull; train
From Rotterdam; to Frankfurt, for their visas.
Consulate closed, gone: they run around, the red tape
Winding, winding round well-disposed advice. On
To Vienna: visas are granted, after
Much filling in of forms, quadruplicate; fees
High, for the British. Be glad, they said,
You're not Japanese.

                The train leaves
About five; reaches the frontier
As the light fades. Coaches are sealed:
One soldier's bulk at every exit.
Czech officialdom comes round: a brusque correctness
Seems just to mask dislike. Slow scrutiny
Of passports, visas, owners; forced cash exchange.
The train lumbers on at last, through darkness
Thick, only broken by red stars on spires
Of villages. After the five hours' wondering,
Arrival: a wooden station like something
Pre-imagined, Russian; so little light;
No steps or stairs, but long wooden ramps.
No Jan to meet us. It is midnight: we wait.
The station sinks back into dark, and quiet.

We find a taxi; cause a resentful tiny
Riot, from what must have been a queue.

We reach the flat Jan half-owns; knock, knock again;
A long and silent wait. The door is opened, narrowly,
By a Bulgarian, still two-thirds asleep; no language
Meeting possible: it's clear only, that
We must go. The taxi takes us
To a large hotel, soon after two a.m.
The room is huge, vast walls, with bare brick
Interstices, some crammed with wires, like springs.
Bugged, we say, as a weak joke;
To haul the spirits up, Zeb leaves his bed,
Puts his head close to the wires, enunciates,
"If this is bugged, you ought to know, this
Is a bloody awful hotel."

          They sleep. At the desk
Next day, Zeb pays the bill, asks
Where the breakfast room is. No.
Is there a coffee bar or something near?
No. They leave, against an eloquent sullen silence.
Just round the corner is a small bar,
Full, at nine a.m.; they drink some coffee.
A tremulous old man comes up to Zeb,
Whispers in English, close to his ear, "This
Is a bloody frightful place. Why do you come?"

          Zeb telephones Jan's sister;
She's careful, monosyllabic; offers
No information; suggests no meeting.

          They find another hotel –
A former brothel for the *Wehrmacht* (officers only) –
Where they're very second-class guests;
Must wait for meals, and twice as long
Should a coachload of the Iron Curtain sort,
Bulgarians or Rumanians, arrive, as they
So often do. Zeb asks if cinemas

Are open Sunday evenings. "Of course,"
Says the desk-clerk with a relish
Almost chewed. "This isn't Britain."

The city is beautiful;
Its restorations exquisite, though you do note
That the new, lovely stained glass in the cathedral
Depicts workers at their lathes, engineers at dams.
We walk for seven days; twenty-five miles
A day; every street covered. We see
The cobbled, timeless beauty:
River, Charles Bridge; Hradcany on its height.
The church where Heydrich's exterminators fought
To their last. Ride the old trams, note the shabbiest
Cars, some doorless, yet seen among the few there are.
The only shiny limousines are for
State police. In the street, below the Castle
Six drive up fast, together. Peaked caps,
Uniforms in khaki; high boots; wine shoulder-boards:
They sprint, orderly, into a building. The street,
Crowded, empties at once, a miracle.

You can buy
Garnets, a bargain; old books, glass. A pub
Has a large room on the street; within,
A smaller; then one smaller yet.
This smallest, almost a dark tiny cave, farthest
From the street, has the most noise,
Most talk.

You sense
A curiosity, a warmth buried, in the crowds;
Held back. You are eyed, and slowly, at some length.
Who might genuinely want a room, have hard currency
To change? Is he the tourist that he seems,
Or a police plant? Avoid all risk; turn away.

Sit quiet at the free, fine concerts in the square.

They go to buy train tickets, for leaving,
At the state travel office. No, not
This one: go to the one that handles all enquiries.
They queue for train details. No, you book
At a third office, across the old town.
They queue there; dutifully stand; almost at the front
After an hour. There is a fascinating
Confrontation. Now, at the counter, is a girl:
Tall, American, blonde, eighteen; from California.
She has been with her boyfriend; has now lost
Her touring group; now wants a train
To Austria. She shouts, pounds desk, refuses
To be put off. "Cut the bus," she snaps.
The Czech girl at the counter, same age, pretty, braided,
Has never heard the like of this tirade; blushes,
Patiently explains the well-worn rules, the sins
Not to be thought of. Cultures clash, head-on
For twenty minutes. Roof echoes; mouths open,
Astonished. The West wins.

                    They pass the time
Until the train, at the new Gottwald
Museum. You don't drop in, walk round here.
You wait for an appointment until a guide
Is free. The helpful young Party man
Shows the approved exhibits; is not too pleased
With questions, especially the wrong ones.
Zeb hopes, bending over the cases,
That this guide will not see the gleam
Of the illegal gold coin he has bought,
Which hangs in his shirt pocket. Too late
To move it. The Russian liberation
Of Prague, is what the large map shows
So vividly: arrows for armies sweeping down

247

From the East. All that's west of Prague, to the Atlantic,
Is either unknown territory, or rests at peace;
No hint of war, or any action there: a blank.

They catch the train
At mid-day, Saturday. As they prepare to board,
A man is dragged off it by seven State police.
He struggles, wrestles, kicks; screams; is frog-marched
Away. Do you, as I, wonder where he is
Now? Before the train moves out, officials
Come, to look for children, being smuggled out,
Under the seats; search expressionless, grave, meticulous.
The seats are rather less than seven inches off the floor.
We leave. The border has all its orthodox
Fitments: barbed wire; a tower with lights and guns;
A few small graves of the unlucky ones.
The journey's over: we saw
Some twisted loveliness, thwarted.

Two months on,
In America, Jan explained. Yes,
He did have his visa, after the years
Of trying. At the frontier, they'd simply
Said that it would not be honoured,
And turned him back. He gave his sister's
Apologies, with his own. When Zeb had telephoned
In his bad German, she'd thought he well might be
One of the State police, or working for them.

No need for apologies.
Zeb had seen and heard: something
Now unavailable. You shall not go
To the place that was. It had
A time-limit on it.

248

124   IV

G.D.R.: to Dresden, 1984

The train crossed Europe. Zeb was met
At Erfurt by his friends;
Driven to Tabarz. They stayed
With the elderly lady who had seen it all
Since the Kaiser; a great square solid house
Of twenty rooms, high, shaped by Franz Josef's age;
Set in lawns, where lay the great hotel
Owned by the family, before the war.
A massive wreck of many rooms;
The long balcony collapsed; abandoned
By an exhausted peace, a government; no windows left;
Roof open to the sky. You clung to
Fallen beams, at grotesque angles, to see
Old spacious rooms, floorless, to a weedy pit
Below. Ghosts, of the 'twenties, Nazi,
Otherwise, hung in the air, over decay;
All now a claim for compension, title,
If you can see beyond the red tape leading
To paralysis.

        The first morning
Fine, July. Jan took Zeb to register
With the police. No words needed
From Zeb; he's inspected, cursorily,
His file opened. Nothing offensive;
Stasi hardly there, inside the uniforms.

        Outside, the little town
Summer-slept. They called at the bicycle shop;
Nothing for sale; this is for repairs: the long
Social chat; a grave discussion, then
Considered estimate: one routine
As good as any other to form reality;

249

The business serious, not minor; the man
Had his life there, in the shop; wanted, asked
No more. No bicycles for sale – nearly nothing
In any sort of shop. The florist's
Is an empty room with three dusty jars
Of dried growth. Do flowers not grow
In the East? The town half-sleeps;
Nothing of menace here; no cars
To speak of. Lunch, solemnly booked
At the restaurant; the waiters young, grave;
Food decent, and served with ceremony, distant;
The faces immature, without energy; aged by black coats,
Bow ties. All is quiet, contained, remote; content
Because unperturbed by hope. The family
Outings, the stroll in the small green park,
With ice cream as the climax – all
That can be expected; life without petty crime;
Nothing to steal. It is the 'thirties;
Even, even the 'twenties. Zeb warms to that.

They play tennis, roll the courts
By the river; before, and – trusted, conscientious –
After. No one fails, or renages. Walk, evenings,
Along the green escarpment path
Where the seat is: survey the whole valley,
Hill-forests. Have dinner, drinks, talk.
No change is in this air: the shock
Lies in wait, quite concealed.

They spend a day
In Weimar: time frozen in symmetry;
The eighteenth century still more alive
Than the twentieth. The immense, weighty
Calm, of Goethe, Schiller *Haus*;
Philosophy made in another age,
And rendered solid, ageless.

Drive out to Buchenwald:
The straight approach-road; space, trees;
Enter: try to think; try not to think
Of distant predecessors, not even ghosts
Now. See the clearing, vast; with the foundations
Of lines of huts; a congruent plan relating
To past, to future, hung between
In no man's land: the exhibitions,
Reconstructions, aimed too carefully to be
More than a gesture. The mind
Cowers away, unstimulated; boggles at larger things
Inside, not outward.

Zeb's friends rise at dawn
To drive the miles to Erfurt: put him
On the train. Leipzig passes, in half-sleep;
Dresden by ten: a great space outside
The station. A long mall to walk
Into the city: dull, spare shops;
The bareness; after the last shock-wave,
A sad sepia dust hanging in the air,
Over the baroque traces, the buildings,
Rebuildings, done in part, restored
Just so far. Regret, regret hangs as spectre
Over the place; deepened to lament
By the changeless things: the lovely
Moated treasure-house, where old beauty
Surfeits, near-sickens; the broad river
That could not burn; the bridge
Spans carnage and nature. Zeb walks
To the square with the cathedral-wreck, *Frauenkirche*,
Piled as some devil Ayers Rock; man-made,
Its blood drained now, leaving
Dinosaur bones. The Butcher's
Statue would blend well, here,
To lord it, over that pile, achieved.

251

Berlin, 1984

The train stops unexpectedly, towards evening
At a tiny station; it could be
Any countryside, flat, green: this, somehow
A little worn, tired: too many lives
Like grazing cattle, have passed here.
Not a scheduled stop; an unexpected pause
Extended, to muse things over. The train
Shambles on; in the end, *Friedrichstrasse*.
Zeb walks to the corner, turns down
Unter den Linden: heavy buildings, chiselled fronts,
Seeming deserted. So is the border, the line.
Wide space, great gate the mind confirms; a different
    world beyond.
No people walk in the summer's late light.
It fades into the quiet. Zeb walks
Back to the station, to face the checkpoint.
Line up in bright glaring light; wait;
Look at each other; each foreign, to all; wait;
The flipped passport; wordless scrutiny,
Brief; relief, with an unaccountable guilt.
Take the *S-Bahn*; this could almost
Be London, before the night starts.
Walk over green space to the isolated 'phone;
Be welcomed at the *Bundesallee* luxury flat;
Host must leave later for a jazz festival
In Holland; hostess will stay; pleasant,
Quiet, correct. At midnight, they drive
Zeb to the shops. It is a permanent fair, raucous,
Too much, piled floor to ceiling, blindingly
Lit; something not real about this luxury.
This exhibition, boast, blandishment eyes you:

The U.S. multiplied by three. The West
Brags, lures, beckons.

          He walks, always walks;
Not pursuing now, nor driven; but open
To the ghosts. Is this the bridge where
Bormann, near the tank, staggered that night,
Fell into mystery? Myths wait at every corner
To be recognised. The present fights back,
Covers; attracts the senses, cavorting, whore-like.
The *Ku'damm*: walk, up and down;
Long always, tired, for the one more stroll
Past the great church, stark, black, attacked
Around its base by cinemas; pass
The cars, parked, and for sale.
Take lifts, down and up, in the *Ka-de-We*:
Cathedral, consecrating longing, wanting, earning, taking,
    having;
Its food floor, tower climax, the only place Zeb's seen
That could make you surfeited, more, sick
With looking. These are superficial
Lures, to kill the myths, but the past
Bides its time, touches across the years.
You chat harmlessly, motiveless, to a stranger
In the restaurant, because this is Berlin, and
You are travellers, on the make, staying alive;
All know this is a phase, and place
In transit, not pausing to be real.

          Tour the city, Zeb. Stand alone
In the Olympic stadium, at the entrance,
To hear the silence speak, the roar
Of the dead, deafen. Climb the wooden horse
To overlook the Wall: gape, awestruck,
Hypnotised, at the Forbidden. The monster, space,
Grey, is as large, almost, as fear.
Regard the *Reichstag* gazing, black, at your slightness;

Saying only *Dem Deutschen Volke*, before
Its impassivity says more.

The Russian monument
Is set back, a miniature: soldiers posture, distant
Automata, altering nothing, hardly existing, saying all
Must change; they, with Zeb. He walks
The Zoo park; the animals are new, among beast-
    ghosts. Note,
On the boulevard, the six-foot shapely blonde awaiting
Customers: striking. She could have exorcised
The She-shadow. Could have; could have.

He has
Gone off each day, all day;
Come back in the small hours,
Imagination sated, numbed with a past
More than half-sought. There are chances,
Half-chances. Zeb finds it easier, though
Not easy, to resist. The old Zeb wilting
Before the new: what is not done.
With hours left, he sees something
Of his hostess, knows her a little.
They see a film, *The Fall of Berlin*,
Only because he wished it. She sees him
Off, at the Zoo station: regret
Wars with routine; hold; do what is planned.
Leave divided, like the city
That's inside him; like this new weariness,
This giving in, before he ever saw it.
How leaden the dividings that this city brings!
Leaving, he does not know this shadow, now:
Das Lied ist Aus.
No photograph, no thing noted,
No glancing half-tune, helps him to know
What the song was.

254

Zeb
Has just read
The diaries
H. Nicolson did;
Feeling, as others do,
He's a bit weak, but
Reports interesting things,
Too.

Churchill, in 'forty five
Still talked of
"The massed majesty
Of the British Empire."
Harold himself hated niggers
He says (I do quote literally), but injustice
(Whatever that is) more. And P.M.
Macmillan, in 'sixty, saw
That Russia would become next
More bourgeois (all these
Remarks, of course, here well out
Of context).

But what perturbs
Zeb's curious mind is: when you sit
As Harold did, at dinner, next to Valerie Hobson
Profumo, and are married to
Sackville-West (Vita),
Both long horse-faces,
One beautiful, one with
"Tomato cheeks, ... thick black moustache"
(Which shows, there's nothing wrong
With horses),
He does not say, but
What did he think?

At the Darlington *v.* Cardiff City
Game, some years ago,
Behind the goal, two policemen stood;
One saying to his mate,
"Surely, goalkeeping here, late
Of Arsenal and Everton,
It is George Wood."

"No," said the other of the duty pair
"That cannot be. I'd know George anywhere."
So they disputed, back and forth
As followers will; until one, confident, impatient,
Lacking a programme, raised his voice, loud
Above the general buzz of expectation;
Turned, appealing to the crowd.

"Can anyone tell me
Who the Cardiff goalkeeper may be?"
No answer yet: merely a muttered babble;
Then, this subsided, a clear, most cultured voice
Placed well back in the rabble
Rose, far above the dirt
And din: obliging tones, the soul of courtesy,
Articulating beautifully, all euphony: "Why,
Certainly, Officer, certainly; a pleasure.

It's that fat prick
In the green shirt."

If you're poor,
In need of cash
Then have a bash:
Seduce, if poss.,
The spouse
Of a rich boss.

And she will bring
Without a ring
Some half (not
To be too much the optimist)
Of what he's got (or
Had) with her, to you,
According
To the new law.
And so you'll be
No longer poor.

Zebulon
Has been such an one
For collecting things.

False jewels and rings,
Coins, stamps, and books
(First eds. and other),
Pewter and silver, cameras, clocks,
Pictures, copper, shells and rocks;
Furniture, maps, and rather
Old newspapers, music boxes;
Ladies (ivory and real), porcelain, brass;
Weapons, medals, war things, glass.

What is his point?
They'll all be sold
When Zeb has gone
To help dogs, old
To have a bone,
And other things.

They lift the heart,
Soothe eyes, and touch
Something inside, that is a part
Of timelessness, and much
Beloved. They do not change, or mule
Or puke (ladies as such,
Exception, proving the rule).
Things, old, are always new;
You visit them; they never you.
And so, demonstrably,
Are better than humanity.

Hitler
Had odd ideas
On race manipulation;
Hating Jews,
Keeping blacks in place.
So we, to compensate,
Get after whites:
It's called Reverse
Discrimina-
tion; or (in the U.S.)
Affirmative Ac-
tion.

Hitler
Was very strange
On art,
Loathing
The mods.
So we, by way of
Decency (though this seems hard),
Reject tradition,
Giving the grants
Only to *avant-garde*
Arts, that make *tableaux morts*
Hanging animal parts.

Hitler
Was peculiar
On women;
Holding
Kirsche, Küche, Kinder
Should be their lot;
Throughout his years
Discouraged queers.

So we, to show we're late ones,
A different regimen,
Attack the men;
Especially
The straight ones.

Zeb's heard it said
(Although aside)
We may have been
On the wrong side.
He tries to think,
Not wishing
Insurrection,
That's just a bit
Of over Correction.

Travel again, but this time, willed,
Moored from home, deliberate.

Landed, they wait, in light snow;
Underfoot, enough to slip on.
The building plain, stucco, floodlit.
Line up with passports for wordless
Confrontation; faintly hostile, no more.
Bus to the hotel; little to see
But broad streets, deserted, in deepening dark.
Shops, perhaps, but no shop windows
Unless oddly small. The hotel
Is huge, new, modern-depressing
Style, shadowing the great open square,
Overlooking gaunt rows of heroism – statues
(One line military, one civilian)
That mark the limits of a war
Remembered, as past corpses are,
Only half-underground. Above,
The buses, busy, ply their circuits:
Crowds, dark specks on white,
Mill round the bus stops.
Seeming casual, eyes examine you
At the hotel entrance. The place is cosmopolitan:
All nations, but the Russian: no mixing,
Not in this hotel. Rooms are standard;
Some close, some high, distant; hundreds, all
The same; the head spins, lacking bearings
As you search them out. Modern-spacious-
Adequate-depressing, is the style.

There are shops nearby
On the wide boulevard. Crowds, pushing, cold,

Walking, breath visible: they pile together, curious,
    immobile
If a consignment, shoes or overcoats, has come in.
Goods, shops, lights, people all seem set
In some poor district, in the nineteen-thirties.

A lad, eighteen
Or so, asks Zeb, politely, if he may practice
His English. He has impressive colloquial
Phrases, American, but has some trouble
In receiving plain sentences.
We chat, pass on. He tracks us,
Reappears: would Zeb consider
Taking a note outside the country
To a girl in Chicago? He met her
On her tour to Leningrad, and is far gone.
He cannot come to the hotel,
Being Russian. Zeb says he needs
To think, but may come down
To the bus stop in the square
At nine p.m. The lad's been home;
Is waiting, with his note. They speak
By a seat between the shrubs of lawns
At the side of the hotel. It looks
Seamy enough, Zeb thinks, to get them
Arrested in London, let alone here.
The note's a gossamer, touching thing:
A pressed flower; some Shakespeare lines.
Days on, it is sent to Chicago
With Queen's head stamps. Zeb returns
To the hotel; looks down
To the square. The 'phone rings;
He answers. Silence. Soon, down there
The gleaming black limousine rushes
Up to the hotel front below.
The figure, jackboots, cap, official,

Hurries in. The wait is long.
Zeb finds, later on, that door
Led to the restaurant.

What is this place? It is water,
Canals, light; spires, slim, in gold; slippery snow.
Great gilted stairways, in the palaces;
Streets of Raskolnikov sets;
Figures, far off, chipping at Neva ice
To bathe or fish.

                    It is the woman,
Shy, pleasant, on Nevsky Prospekt, with the baby
Strapped like a mummy in the tiny sleigh.
She pulls it to a halt, smiles her permission;
Waits gracefully for the photo that
Never does come out. It is the Palace
At Pushkin, with the long snow-slippery walks
And the new Versailles gilt inside.

The train for Moscow is dusty,
Old; eight hours as light slowly fades
To dark: trees and space, space,
Endless trees; shabby wood houses
That could have been Canadian,
Had they seen paint in forty years.
All moves past, fronting the cavernous
Emptiness; all details still, changeless;
Only the day alters, failing.

There are old wooden houses
In streets preserved as antiques
In Moscow, but only in rare places.
The circus is an opera, serious; audience awed.
One section for Generals, overweight, set in rows

Like their own medals. Even the laughter
Is solemn.

                    Moscow cliché scenes
Are satisfactory: the ochre British Embassy
By the river: across, the Kremlin, Eastern,
Medieval. The sleek black limousines
Of government, important, race down wide streets:
The Arbat, where you walk free at any hour;
No mugging here; not yet. Its shops
Are pity-poor beside the shaming
Lushness of the tourists'
Hard currency stores. Incongruity
Is the new Olympic stadium seen from heights
Over the city.

Inspection of documents, routine: lights
From the mirror, angled precisely above,
Dazzle your eyes. Officials do not speak;
Merely mutter between themselves;
Gaze, gaze expressionless, blank
Until set minima of intimidation are
Achieved; then, you may leave. Are these
The ends of foreign policy?

One more part of the planet
Has been viewed; and beyond that
Sensed. Reality greets imagination,
And, like some good teacher, corrects,
Then stimulates. Other journeys
May be conceived, and willed
As this. It makes no difference whether
They come from travel, books or vision.
Once born, they shall return, just as this,
To the centre: this place

Of belonging, this garden
Where I watch the universe,
And am slowly changed.

The dread old partnership.
Loins, triggering longing brain, stirred yet again.
I know that women, when in harmony
Can, making fire from rock, like Gonne
Light up, effloresce
Beyond their rivals fire and sun;
And that poets claim so.
But I, I have the photographs I took
(Subject at fifty-two) that prove – see this same book –
Enough remained to shake and frighten you,
When rooms she entered, changed to sun and light.

Prices are there to be paid.
Seasons, looking the same as they appear,
Amass their hidden bill of rue.
Now, old, I have a wife.
Stone rubs with fellow-stone.
I wish I had a dog again,
Or even two.

When Boro are away
Zeb watches Whitby Town;
Where the old pensioner is: handsome-worn,
Gentle-man, near, in the stand, with his dog,
Benjie, who has troubled Zeb
Since the start; seeming the ghost, just once removed,
Of Zeb's old Branwell: black, tan-silky, sad eyes
Alert; now long dead, loving, loved.

This one was kicked by a lout;
Symbol, pride of his times, no doubt; comprehensively
Educated, life well adjusted to his days;
Kicking most comprehensively too,
Kicked Benjie's eye near out.
So the dog watches play one-eyed,
His head turning, where the ball is
(More than half the field at goal-kicks),
Far more attentive than the crowd.

At half-time he devoured two quarters
Of Zeb's sandwiches, Zeb the other two.
(His master, last year, sent a Christmas card);
Before his car packed up, marooning him
In the dead industry-shell up the coast,
And he and Benjie far too proud for help.
There is, now, space where Benjie was,
Where Zeb is lost, reduced
Merely to watching Whitby Town,
In the Northern League.

Miss Short, M.P.,
Does not wish us to see
On page three
Any hanging free.
And when she
Who, I think, has two,
Appears on TV,
Will not countenance one,
It seems mean to me,
Does she think
We want three?

I looked up
Above my garden gate
At a sheep
Up the bank, opposite,
Across the road,
At the wire fence;
Head on, backed
By the sun-sky.

I looked at him.
He, at me.
He, unsheared, bulky, on thin legs,
Chewed casually,
In perfect silhouette.

I must have looked,
Lit by his sun,
A possible god;
Well, at least interesting,
Mildly.

We stood unmoved,
Knowing, the importance of it.
He held his ground.
I gave up mine.
Did he care
As we gazed,
At all, for me
As I do now, for him?

Possibly.
It's a big sun-sky space
He's left in the fence
Now he's gone.

269

No more of this.
You summoned me. Now
There shall be
No more half-promises,
Half held back;
Half-givings, made
Half absent-mindedly.

I will be mine again, be
The one I know;
Free to go
To lust in peace;
Love-lust grown hate-lust, relief
Under sky other than this,
Coughing its snow.

NINETEEN NINETIES

One instant, and in mists, brought
To the man-animal a thought.
Not mere instinct for food, hunt,
Enemy, cunt. Free of his eye, his head
Saw things that grew, moved, altered;
Saw sky; dark, light.
Some sight, leapt
Sudden within the head,
Touched, once, with stars:
A curiosity born, an awe
Forced him, on cavern walls, to draw;
Ages on, to write.

Monks would enscript such awe in gold,
Blue, red. Men spoke, doubting, athirst;
Argued, brought evidence; cited
The texts. Unaware, they were first
Scholars, being a kind of college, then
University. That word, the word!
Seeking to know a universe, cherishing
The Knowing: at the heart ever, unperishing,
Imperishable, the books. Scholars, they urged
Young ones to see, as Plato had, in the far age,
Calling it teaching. Teaching could sing.
They tried, some young, to build upon
The books, to force thought on;
To doubt, refuse, think again, brook
No certainty: re-search (the word again).
Universities, at last, with these two trusts:
Teaching. Research:
Built always on the flowing of the books.

Millenia do not kill, but
The tempting, the old fork, is

273

There yet. Shoot the Albatross.
Desire is otherwise: not for the Knowing, now,
But species-ego: humans the core; universe near
Nothing, men the all. *Homo sapiens* –
Sapiens? New sub-god, that lacks a better.
Man, now: his rights, comfort-suborned, unlettered;
All that is physical; for all as gift.
Men equal. All the illusions.
If any one should be too palpable,
Shouting denial in the face,
Pretend: act
As if equality were fact.
If god there might have been,
Grant him an off-day, a
Failure to complete an order,
Forgetting – Derelict! – to make equality in men.
Men must do his failed task for him, then.
Form a party, and proceed:
Lo! Man is no more a little miracle,
Mystery, set in greater skies;
Let him be social, a yob
As good as any in the football mob.
A social-*Ism*: the word, ever, reveals: descent
To Lowest Same. *Circumspice*:
See it in buildings, clothes and faces, cars,
Television, food, sex, film stars –
The Same:
Shequality – sham – shoddy shame.

If you trace back this foetid stream
To source, you reach Rousseau
And the inherent nobleness of Man, a dream
Which you know (so do I)
Runs counter to experience
Being a simple lie.
But never mind; pretend

274

That with the alleged goodness comes intelligence,
Of which there's, too, a limitless supply
At any given time.
If you believe that, stop reading. Go
Away; for that's the super, nuclear lie.

But that is so upsetting, hence
Pretend it isn't so.
Claim brains are commonplace;
And all we need
Universities, more, then more again; for more
Heads; it is no matter if they scarcely read.
And if we can't afford
More universities, why, Lord,
If we want better heads,
Change names: Leicester Poly to
De Montfort U.; and the expense
Just a few pounds for letterheads.

Come off it. An infinite supply
Of intelligence, potential,
Is hot air.
It isn't there.
Intelligence is rare.
More means worse, and that shall be: therefore
Hansard-pretend: "... the numbers entering
Higher education ..." – always increasing, ever increased,
May mask the truth that learning
Is nearly ceased.
Nerve connections in the brain
Result from genes, through chance, and learning.
Not much to do about the genes
Or about chance, both
Faits accomplis, causes for yearning.
But O, the learning!
Try to conceive one current curse

Without its root in learning-lack,
If you should doubt
Enormity of loss.
Not quite dead yet?
Embezzle the poor ignorant
With fraud-parchment.
Remember, remember, hearts of universities
Used to be books, that came from mind.
Be rid of the books: leave no trace behind
Of the books, the books, to win this war.
Burning will do no more.
Burning was tried,
Failing to kill.
Replace! Replace!
Drown first, drown. Drown them, the books,
In ignorance. Sea-ravaging, ignorance cannot know
Where next to go; or even that it is so.
Pack the curricula of youth
With pseudo-newdo cults, the easy treat.
Should there be an escape, some leak
In attainment of final solution,
Have the new pundits bury it
In scholar-speak.
Dissonance; all relative;
No good-bad-better-best,
No fail, no pass;
There shall be no truth;
Can be no test.
If you do teach, teach *Coronation Street*.
Use, use the "universities":
Place the failed scholars at controls,
Oiling-administering the joints,
Checking the gauges, staying out of trouble.
Universities are instruments; they must be
Bulldozers, machines

276

To level, press
To equal rubble.

The circle drawn
Complete: this journey over.
Men back, as before the first awe struck,
First need to know, first lover.
The turning point? An abcess
Burst, pus overflowed, drowned mind
Along with courage, in the Black Deathade.
Darkness has been made
Again, war won; and from
Some old monk's grave, protrude
Few spongy perforated bones, dried
In casual wind.

After? Rhythms gather all:
There are such things
As pendulums, metronomes,
Graphs, cycles. Might there be
Curiosities reborn, new Comings?
If the old crime
Have not killed utterly
The seeming speck of green
In the dead plant. That may well be gone.
Even if not, one degree
In arc of metronome lasts,
Lasts longer, far, than any
One life
Can be.

Zeb dislikes clubs;
Since clubs
Are groups of folk,
Committee-run,
Pigs in poke,
They must be duds.

Take
Yorks. C.C.
Who decide, after
Careful referenda
(Results not
What Committee required)
To surrender
Heritage, that
Was unique;
To leave
(For Aussie bowler,
Then Indian bat)
The timeless thing
They can't retrieve.

Or take Archbish
Of Cant.
(A large club, his,
Though often
Hit for six
And shrinking);
He's now quite big, raving
Away, in politics,
But rarely thinking;
Had his own envoy
(Lost him a spell,
But with free bed

And board – a saving).
This same Archbish –
Stipend not small –
Has had a whine
At salaries (biz).

Zeb would he'd been
The joining sort;
More social, communal;
So could resign
And sod them all.

I

Come to the House of Automata.
See what they can do.
Some have names like Bobbety and Menzies;
But all have thingies, and make more sound
Than dolls that utter cries;
These carry labels, and wear funny ties.
A buttonhole touched, these well-whipped men
Can move, throw papers, cry Hear-Hear,
Smile (Fawning or Knowing)
At what is right
Or Left, these well-whipped men;
Stretch skeletons straight;
And sit down again.

II

These are the very latest prizes
Of research: they breathe, take in stale air, and taste
What is ingested; perform digestion's falls and rises,
And skilfully expel most genuine waste
Almost entirely from the mouth. The cheaper ones
Do not undress, and even our better quality
Not in public; all behaving, superficially
At least, conventionally; not to be
Distinguished, not with ease
From genuine live ones.

III

Creeping-contorting to catch three eyes:
Camera, Minister, Speaker (in order),
Delivering on cue the question planted,
Raised in best dung and unction extreme: –
Will my Right Hon. Friend not agree
That all that he has said

Is just so, just so, so right, so true;
Though possibly
Even he, so right, so blue
Or red, may not quite see, to a degree,
How much his fine correctness
Delights and transports me
Beyond orgasm. And can he not see
That, in my far smaller way,
I am almost as right as he,
And thus, for future, mark
My utter suitability?

IV

What moves them all? Try science,
Analytic calculation. One affair, in the SD
(Not *Sicherheitsdienst* – Social Democrats)
One connection, grown too social,
Wins poll-percentage points: 3.
The mathematical, like me,
Divide the Grail of Fifty-One-Percent by 3.
Ergo, to swing one election
Takes 17 seductions.

V

Is this the best that we can do?
Are these, these few,
Representatives, icons of the breed,
The best, the best that we can do?
It may well be, since
The fewer yet, of flawed humanity,
Marred by flecks of decency,
Cursed with a quaint integrity,
Would never touch the parties or the place.

VI

Well, roll the cameras, sail on ship

281

Of state, and wield the whip.
Flourish the bought ambitious laugh.
I could, almost, believe them real
If I might view
From Strangers' Gallery
Just one M.P.
Who would step back and laugh
At what they do.

If we'd wanted to be in Europe,
We should have thought before
To have kept the Americans over there,
So we could have lost the War.

We rather let the poor Czechs down
In nineteen-thirty-eight.
But we rallied round the Poles, when they'd
The Germans through the gate.

After quite a bit of trouble
And considerable sin,
We saw the Germans out
As we let the Russians in.

The Czechs are still complaining
At what we chose to do;
But it turned out fair and equal.
They got the Russians too.

Then the Russians fell to pieces.
Czechs and Poles both gained a lot;
And we're left now contemplating
The next steps of the gavotte.

Last night on TV Zeb heard them say
They had no use for Olivier.
He's a few years dead, so it's right on cue
That they assemble, communally to screw
Him. Their major moan appeared to be
(If Zeb could discern it from sound
They made) was: his acting was wrong way round.
Should have been from inside out, they claim;
Not outside in – well, it may have been
The other way round; anyway, it came
From a direction they couldn't approve.
How they discerned the route he'd taken
To where he'd arrived, was not explained.
And he couldn't say, being dead too.
But they were sure they weren't mistaken
And were a formidable crew.

In command was Russell Davies;
Which surprised Zeb, for R.D.
Writes decently
On sport,
Where he's funny as Kingsley Amis
(Who, wise as ever, wasn't there).
There was a man called Bog
Danov, who spoke on cuts (not comic);
Another called Trader
And one named Snoo;
And a weighty one from York U.
Called Hermione Lee, a feminist She,
Zeb would bet. Alan Brien ran the critical rule
Over Sir Laurence – or was that Brian Allen?
There is so much the wrong way round
Nowadays; on stage, in school.

Which reminds – O yes, there were
Some real sixth-formers from Westminster,
Who'd brought their teacher along.
There were clips of Sir Laurence, all sound
And fury, with some high-pitched.
But, years dead, he's no way of knowing
That he should have been coming when he was going.

I saw, at a distance,
A man leave the farmhouse
Carrying a blue bag
Up into the field, against the cloud.

And, after, the sheep ran
Against the horizon,
Stampeding, crowding, always running,
Save the slow, odd stragglers.
I hoped no dog was driving them.

There was no dog:
Just the last few sheep.
Then they too jostled, then ate
Towards evening.
So: all lives, condemned,
Do have their moments.

There was a time
Zeb had his friends;
Some Jews, some blacks;
Liked them, and never thought
At all about it:
Drove carefully, and never trussed
Himself into his car;
Reported income, conscience-free;
Knew no one could doubt it,
For tax.

Now there's the Race Relations Act,
And that on Seat Belts:
Front Act first, then Back;
A new bit on the tax return
That says, it's not enough
To tell the truth, re.
Interest gained; now, by laws
You must obtain, and then report
How building socs. and banks
Arrived at it; detail their sums
As well as yours.

Unfair,
It seems to Zeb, to have
Performed on him a mind-change op.
Without consent, implanting
Political incorrectness; revamping,
Making him over. How unfit it is
To turn him into Bigot, stamping:
made in G.B. Patents: –
Race Relations Board, and
Parliamentary Committees.

Why have stars, film and TV,
Now become so uggely?
They used to be
Like Tyrone P.
And Grace Kellee.
We had Boris Karloff, one needs
To concede,
But he didn't play romantic leads.

But now, there's one, I see,
With little holes where
Bits of face should be,
And Ruby waxes fat
On TV.
And Edison Ghoul
Whose face is there, but long, long,
Bloodhoundish, but a most sick
One.
Is it that they're supposed to be
The average manwomanperson, he-she,
So we won't feel bad, now
Being all the same? No,
No; if so, they've over-corrected.
And how.

Zebulon would rather go
To bed with Tyrone P.
In his present state
(Dead since '53)
(And Zeb is straight),
Than any She

With cracks, and holes
Dalmationly.

I've noticed that some girls are made
All sinewy, like Lavinia Spade.
Capable, yet, of pulling a whistle;
But still, all bone, taut muscle, gristle
Like that rejected at a butcher's shop:
Slim, set, mean, and carved like rock;
(Another one is Darlene Block).

Beware. Protect your guided missile.
Do stop and think; for some like these
Would draw you in – soul, body, rissole –
While with a lustful joy they shout.
These don't do things by halves;
And, once around your back, their calves
Would crush your spine in frantic sin,
And never, never let you out.

A father shot the man
Who'd killed his son.
Case came to court: the jury found
Him innocent. The sounds
Of shock were loud. Editorials
Lectured, prim, severe. However sore,
Juries (preached the *Sunday Tele.*) must go by law
Just as it is, not what they feel
It ought to be.

      Yet law
Relies on precedent. I've heard
It wasn't quite like that
When powers-that-be, met busily
At Nuremberg.

Zeb never liked her much; she
Never had his vote.
Too chill, too cut-and-dried; low voice
Suggesting intimacy; questionable, then remote.
After she died, they went through
Schell's film; then the standard concert:
London, 'seventy two;
Sets pink, she in fur; songs near spoken;
Regular, certainly well-worn; popular, best.
Monotony unbroken:
Cole Porter, *Lola*; *Falling in Love Again*
And the rest.

Yet Zeb just once
Heard her sing a German song
Of parting: *Das Lied ist Aus.*
He never heard the like, never
A song to shatter so; voice
Violent, broken with pain:
"*Wir gehen auseinander ...*" –
Defiant, tragic: one single note, one moment
Did touch that, not heard again.

Zeb pleads with you to look
To find it; listen; is glad to give
This tip, to you, for reading
At least this bit
Of his book. (If Zeb were dead,
And could, he might be pleased
With such a thing
From someone who
Did not much like him.)

Now (sorry: at this moment in time),
Now, tennis hunks
Look like stamp collections,
Or much-travelled trunks.
Cricketers afield
Are beer bottles, sealed
And not on tap,
With neat trade names,
Bass, Tetley Bitter, each side
Below the cap.
Now, no one runs fast
Or wins his race.
He just supplies
An injection of pace.

Old shots and shoot
Now strikes and strike;
Forwards are strikers;
Names on shirts
(Shirts now strip)
And shirts themselves,
Expensive folly,
Change each season
For the lolly.

They say, though before thinking,
You can't split sport
From politics,
These being an indissoluble mix.
Yet politics consists
Of rant,
And cant;
Both stinking.
Defy what they say:

294

You could go back
Any time, any day,
Perform a fix
On politics:
Omit the rant,
Sort out some cant,
Without being prissy;
Get rid, by neat selection,
Without distortion
Some smaller portion of
Hypocrisy.

There was no need to cancel
To please Hain's lot
Cricket tours to S.A.
On the very same day
United took to the air
For Communist Kiev
(A bastion of freedom
From prejudice there!)
You could introduce a quite obsolete touch
Of live-and-let-live;
Even face the fact
That folk have a mind, set much
To congregate
With their own kind.

You could have done the odd small flips
With Europe's football championships:
Let a Jugoslav team that had qualified, play,
No matter what the U.N. say;
Instead of throwing the kid right out,
And kicking his marbles away.
It's true fate made that one backfire;
And the Danes, away
On holiday, unqualified,

Came in; taught us how to play,
And won. Hooray!
                    If that miracle be,
You too could go back
Just here and there, perhaps in bits;
Drop fragments of hypocrisy,
Odd corners of the politics.

A tiny thing alighted, sudden, there
Upon the page I read.
I tried to flick him gently to the air
Surrounding. I was clumsy: he was dead.

He left a minor smudge upon the page.
I wet my fingertip to clear the text.
Then, in my guilt, I saw his life, his age,
Should not pass unrecorded, unappreciated.

So, leaving the one speck unmolested,
I turned the page; read on. Each self
Has been unique. The book, completed,
Is now back on its shelf.

Late dawn: two young deer, real, not ghosts in mist,
Were on the back lawn; from the woods;
Confident, exploring, nuzzling the old birdseed
From the grass: like large goats, surprisingly
Solid – nothing ethereal; their brown a deep brown.
Photographed, they saw the flash
With interest, and never ran. Young, young.
One moved out of sight, to explore the house-side.
When he returned, to close, gladly, with his mate,
You could feel the warmth of it.

But the one left limped, hung the front hoof
In the air, a pendulum. The food was near
Nothing: Zeb, helpless to help. Had he approached,
Taken out food, love, anything, they and the wonder
Would have flashed, melted back, fey,
Into the woods. So, powerless, human-like,
Estranged, he went back to bed. He has lost
In his time, several friends that way.

There was a creature on our bathroom wall.
He stayed all through my bath;
Brown, indeterminate, stationary, small
(I do apologise to the appropriate authority –
He may have been a she, or she a he;
I deny sexism; the determinant was far
Too small to ascertain at all,
Since her/him I could hardly see entire.)
My wife will come and place it on the lawn,
Perturbed, and uttering sympathetic conversation.
It will wonder why all's turned so green and cold,
Missing the steam, and ignorant that her
Affection is a modest and involuntary step
In Natural Selection;
Contributing a mite to Wildlife Conservation.

Words must re-make
What's in the head.
To tell, seek words
As best you may.
Words make the thing:
The equation's set.
Only then
Comes the paid debt.

Acts of faith
Govern the choosing;
Meaning's inside.
Right words
Stay the losing.

The sin's
To do otherwise.
Truth to truth
Is within:
Absence of lies.

Trends, fashions tempt
The easy way;
A welcome guest.
Seize, grip your truth;
Die, maybe, trying.
Obscurity's dust,
Lying.

Easy to
Pose, perplex:
Cover the flaw
With words piled loose;
Smother corpse-rot.

300

At best, intimidate;
Worst, force escape.
There was right meaning, high,
Low, at your beginning.
Now, you lie.

Lie, if you dare.
Those who do –
Gone, going
Not for recalling.
The bargain's hard:
No rewards, even
For those who try.
Writing's a falling.

Think of Maugham:
Clarity, euphony,
Reason, routine.
Old after his time;
Shrouded, hiding,
Collapsing, wild:
The shell of him
Shrivelling, danced
In the fire, riding.

Yeats, life's love lost,
Thought of a daughter;
Took the treatments,
Took to politics.
A lie.
A shrinking there.
Pass by.

Frost: Zeb heard him
Chant his poems
One Harvard day.

301

Bronzed, creased, New England grey;
Dying songs, poignant,
Trailing; a pity-voice
Echoed away.

One, younger, died: Lay
Your Sleeping Head.
The ravaged face
Disintegrated.
He's a blue plaque
On the house wall
Zeb passes, on the way
To see York City
Try to play.

Friend, lover, China mate:
Charming schoolboy
In his fifties, with
The cow-lick hair.
Friendly, unspoiled;
Issuing invitation
Too late.

Ill-named, Snow
Who sought to bridge
The science gap.
A red-faced chap
Who came to lunch.
Ghastly, isolate,
Unwilling to communicate;
Brings his wife, who'll wear
Novel intellect and upswept hair.
What was he like?
A colleague asked
(Expectant, curious, taut):

Well, he was
Nasty, British, and short.

Find no despair in this, nor hate.
Tell your truth
In simple words, right words;
Faith chooses straight.
It is your very self:
No profit in it. It will
Grant no advancement, nor
Ameliorate your end.
It does you no favours.
You lived, and here.
Let it stand.

Brown remote mountains frown in mist.
Nearer, green-gold-green reeds, below the palms;
All given twice, mirrored in the green glass
We sail on. How can it be,
That these, under the occasional bird
Splitting the sky, speak more
About five thousand years
Of toil, of ghost-lives flickering still,
Than do the tombs and monuments?
The gliding of the ship;
The stork against his island frond,
Still, as the river moves
Its panorama on;
Black buffalo graze
On the far side; all arresting time,
Moving only the mind, towards ever.
Eloquence, speaking never,
Says all: here, now, always
Beyond the reaching.

Yesterday I hurried round the pond,
On the flagstones around its edge.
It's a pond that tries to be round,
But has four right-angled corner-bits
Each one a tricky ledge.

Sixty six years back, I ran
Round this stone circuit. I hear yet
A female voice, warning of ill,
To take care, but I forget
Whose voice it was – my mother's
Or the maid's; another's?
I had no trouble then
At corners, dashing around,
Showing off for the huge goldfish,
And the Mercury bronze over the lilies,
In mid-pond on his island ground.

I did well enough yesterday, too:
Slower, with no more than a twinge at thigh
And hip. There was no one else
In the garden, but Mercury watched his pond-fringe
And remembered? Alone, Mercury and I.

All looked the same, precisely,
But for one thing: the goldfish,
They had turned small! Strange!
When most things grow. When I reflect
On the pool, and the stone track,
I think I may have lapped myself,
And am amazed, at the number and range
Of possible reasons for the change
Revealed, by this turning back.

Go back, go back; go
To where self, mind
Are rooted
And can grow.

Having just met, being forty-three,
The stranger, named security,
Zeb stood on the stone bridge;
Gazed steady at the garden
In the sheltered bowl below,
Bisected by the stream;
Looked at the house, solid, firm,
Old stone, long weathered grey,
Lording it, above.
He took his everything, three thousand pounds,
Placed it into the dream,
And went away.

Come back, come back.
Choose village, county,
Country, continent, race:
The very spot
Within, beyond all these.
All fancy, reason, hope, desire
Lead to this place.

This home has waited.
Others paused on the bridge
To gaze, as Zeb had done
When he was ten.
He'd wondered, then,
At some half-dream of order in
Roses, flowerbeds, repose; close trim;

Privacy, distance, peace, power here,
Not for the schoolboy, him.

Also, in the absent years,
Stopping on the bridge,
They must have looked
At wildness, chaos forlorn;
Not knowing that
A continent away,
Seeds to reincarnate
Lay in a brain
To make a home reborn.

Visits made,
Hopes planted;
Love-things gathered, some
Glimpses of home, belonging;
More than two decades
Until the coming home.

Come back, come back.
Seek no more
Better, or worse.
Stand on this spot
To view
The universe.

Fortress, in wars of taking,
A dead place, stirring, was a friend.
The years of isolation have their end.
Give something back, give, in the making.
Room by room, one single
Honest man, himself rooted, trained
In another age, worked
Three years, five years.
Now see a garden and a lawn
Where forests were.

Carved black oak assembled,
Jacobean, in a dining room.
A Georgian sitting room, a bedchamber
Pre-Raphaelite, more or less;
A study walled with books, in alcoves.
Ignore ill purists, irksome
Advisers, theorists at some remove; they guess.
Make one of things you love; come,
Come home.

They still stand on the bridge;
Gaze, now, at order, growth
To harmony. All's done
In seven years. This place
Is my poor mind and soul.
All's set in place, new come;
Past things, felt lovely once,
Desired, and now come home.

Come back.
Set wander-weary feet
To where brain, soul
And body live as one
Until their close;
Circle complete.

Root, flower are sure
Again. This love is given, unaware.
There is no object, nor no single room,
No garden corner, squirrel, bird, or song
Or plant I do not know
At least in shape or form.
In this place we belong.

There are, here, battlements
Guarding a world that ought to be.

I cannot raise my eyes
Without a sight of some loved thing
With memory, placed there for me.
This marriage knows me intimately;
This place has never had a lie
From me. We are alive.

I shall not leave again;
We die together.
As some skeleton that falls
To dust, is soil for some growth, new,
This house may stand again at ease,
Giving, to lives and ways;
Others yet stand on the bridge, and gaze.
But not these days, not these.

Be back, be back
In first green, sun, fall, snow,
To where the seed
Was rooted,
And does grow.

This great and tiny house, made
Near three centuries ago,
Is an accusation; reproving aside
To the stately houses trade.
You see it from the road. Built wide
Around the great raised central door;
Solid, Palladian, firm-pillared; large
Georgian windows stare, but only four.
Approach: the chiselled front, where one peacock calls,
Dissolves, like vagueness in declining eyes.
Sandstone, cut sharp once, now weathered
To roundness; crumbles, falls.

There is no place like this.
The door is open to the wind. Mount steps;
Enter: no soul inside.
The hall is a small room, swept
Through contemptuously by the wind.
On the table, a fine silver box
With entrance-fees and change; say
Does fame, some other age, or shrouding dust
Keep thieves away?

Move through, towards the light:
A dining room, once made
As open Italianate colonnade,
Till the North wind brought sanity:
Glassed in now, a conservatory, forsaken.
The long table, that almost fills
The room, is set for dinner
That never will be taken;
Light half-glints on silver, glass
Where dust sits, mistaken.

Outside, the little lawn
With geese, rises
To the waterfall
From the lake above.
A child's Chatsworth
Surprises.

Pass off the hall:
The bedroom, large, high, square;
Four-poster bed, dusty; and a cradle, away
In a corner: this, fresh white, expectant,
Breaks the decay.
A second, tiny bedroom: old single bed
Collapsing. A cockade hat
Dirt-gilted, on the dresser;
And scarlet uniforms hang; wait
For a military man,
Two centuries late.

The drawing room
Has two great Georgian windows
Peeling, old paint curling.
Books, old, beautifully bound,
Foxed, fading, paining.
On the floor
By the chair that's torn
Is today's *Times*
(Business Section) new, forlorn:
Hopes of gaining.

The lady's there, sudden
Silent, as a spectre:
Apologises for her absence;
Daughter-in-law, expecting,
Rushed to hospital, doctors suspecting
Possible complications.

Hostess is charming,
With the charm outside,
Across familiar gulf
Kept against ordinary others.
She shows us the Empress
Eugenie's chair: brocades
Faded, tattered to ribbons, but hers
Undeniably. The wind is cold;
Logs laid, unlit, in the small fireplace;
For this is summer still, late: also old.

There is no place like this, where
Age and youth join, struggle to hold
It. Is there no cold, no bitterness of air
No other suffering the aristo, choosing,
Will not endure, using
Will, will, to cling on to the place,
To the gulf? Struggle is endless,
Perpetual losing.

Ceilings, once plaster fantasies,
Hang. No gold-rich restoration,
Calculated glitter, here;
No illusion gaudily excites.
Go to the great remakings, National Trusts, for that.
Here, I see time alive, prospering
At work, winning his war of nights
And days, though meeting mad, irrelevant resistance.
No dust, here, is scattered by the wind.
So far, this dust is never quite allowed to fall
To the general dust.
This tries to shroud. Old things
Where through obscurity shines beauty, half-flaunt
Half-hidden loveliness. Oblivion
Shall win. It is the mind, battling, battling to lose:
That, that shall haunt.

I

Above this garden, as I lie
Under the clearest, enigmatic sky,
A little slightly ragged cloud moves by,
Warmed from a sun, blood-red behind closed eye:
Far off, an estranged, half inimical cry
Of some bird; a flutter-patch of butterfly.
The stream persists, now low
With dryness; soon swelled with summer rain.
All is flux, movement; this moment touching peace,
All breathing inward; then reaching for release.
All power, except the power to cease.

II

Blood touches lightly, heavily on the brain; thoughts pass,
Fade, as shadows move along the grass.
Sleep beckons, half in fantasy; harbinger
Of longer sleeps to come. Death is on this air;
Birth; energy, viewed through a microscope.
Scaled otherwise, with equal ground for hope
And hopelessness, a cosmos lightly probed
By radio-telescope.

III

The stream murmuring the only sound
In solitude; evening held
Ambivalent, between the night and day.
Soon the least micro-flash of time
Will show the Milky Way.
The mind has love for what has bound its love:
Love is no catalyst for what the poets dreamt of.
No answer here, no reaching, binding
As one; no rush of breeze, no sense of Whole,

No phantom, even, of a goal; no seeking, finding,
No shadow of a soul.

IV

Creatures I loved
Lie in the earth of continents
Other than this.
Close eyes, ears, against the ebb and flow
Of stream, meandering. Beyond this quiet, know
We are space travellers
Dead or alive: why must
We differentiate the cosmic dust,
The only love we have,
Can hope to find?
I am, shall be, a leaving;
Least fragment of a star
Which held, for once at least,
In time remote past the conceiving,
An unresponsive garden in a mind.

No cliché-candle lying in the dark
For me:
No church, now given to sociology.
But, deep within this body's seas,
Pre-primal, clinging to the rocks,
(Miles down, obscure, this ocean-earth);
Hard, hard this shell:
Within, born since my birth,
The diamond-pearl, black,
Stranger to light and to mortality,
Being one single certainty –
That will not be discussed,
Spurring no words.

Rise, rise now, from sea depths
To the star, surface-suspended:
Mind, brain, trace its galaxy; then on,
On, beyond all stars, rendered
Black holes; beyond
Space and time lost, beyond conceivèd edge
Where no edge is; where brain-leaps
Find vacuum, irrelevance; beyond exhaustions
Where all fails, fails even to perturb;
Where blankness is, and no denial;
Beyond all known surrenders, where possibility
Is not. To there, O far past there, let hurl
Reverberations, answering, from my diamond-pearl,
Black, knowing no light,
And stranger to mortality;
That will not be deterred;
Spurring no word.

I

To finish like Candide, well,
You can't ask more than that.
Zeb's getting fond of gardens
(But not the digging, nor the chat
Of experts); he knows few flower names;
He's never read a text
Horticultural, or botanical.
Still, he notes, this March, that the brown stalks
Have green lumps on.
Now, what will happen next?

II

He was contemplating this, in the garden, in a large
And passive way, when, by some fancy,
Some necromancy,
Or maybe for no reason – none at all –
Imagination probing, out-of-joint;
Sudden, he faced the One-in-Charge,
Who came straight to the point.

III

Would you agree to play it all again?
You've been a lively puppet, and I can't resist a prank.
Be re-born (though not Christian – frank
ly a waste of time, and regimen).
Moreover by this time, with the confidence to prove
Wisdom, from living once (this with an artful smile)
If you repeat, you may improve;
I'll make it worth your while.
Take some roads not taken;
Make right decisions: be free of wives,
Be so much less mistaken.
Get to know more dogs than ever

All their loving lives.
Of trends and fashions be aware
Before they happen – especially in academia.
You'll still have to judge the changes,
For you can't be made quite free:
Your character won't alter; you'll be
Hopeless with women still, old sport,
Nor immunised from ills of various sorts
Like loyalties: which means watching, e.g.,
Scarborough F.C., whose motto, still, will be
No Battle, No Victory.
So you'll sit through
All draws and losses
Yet again.
Well, I shall close, for a swift decision
With an offer that's a treat
No competitor dare match:
A fifteen per cent reduction in the silly sods you'll meet.

IV

Zeb hesitated: it didn't seem a lot.
He took the merest momentary pause
For mature deliberation.
Then, He was back, and on the very spot
Just as before, but sore
Now, and with less accommodation.
You've had all that, that I described before, he said.
It's been two years (by my time),
And no capitulation
To my best offer, generous, from heart and head.
Now, one last chance:
You can still have your lot again
But, this time, just the same.
Two choices only now:
Go through it all once more,
Precisely as it was; in each detail restore

317

The past; no power to improve, amend, or ask
Questions; and, to you, just as before,
Ignorance of what's to be, behind the mask
Inscrutable, of a perpetual future.

Or, there remains
The usual arrangement, set and sealed.
My standard contract, without options, offers: –
We call negotiations off. I leave, as
Of now: and all to be revealed
After the final veil
Has been withdrawn, and all that rot.
Take it or leave; there'll be no other sale,
Much less a special, not
For you.

V

Zeb took a month or two (his time) to think it over thus,
Watching the calendar days pass;
The One even helped him – Celestial Mail, first class –
To make a balance sheet, minus and plus.
You'll get your father and your mother
Over again, just as before, as such;
Beautiful shapes and sizes, antiques, and books;
Friends (in passing); even some love; not much.
You'll get up on your toes and sweep the race
Again, and have your fill of some desiring looks.
The days of Thirties stillness, gold and blue
Once more will seem to last for ever, new
Though now long gone, along
With all the expectations they occasioned.
And even at your end,
The green will still shoot forth from winter brown,
Though less, ever less, to do with you.
But all the very best I save till last:
Dogs, that you loved before, can love again.

VI

One final note of warning: against the taking
Of stupid risks; especially contract-breaking,
Like dying in the midst, before your term be done.
My power could sentence you
To fourteen years of Women's Liberation;
Rolling the Sixties years repeatedly
Uphill, forever Sisyphus,
But worse. Deconstruction, endless books
In Criticspeak, and scruffy blokes with beards, and looks
Of glassy-eyed intensity, fanatics
On multiple committees, chaired by you,
Running, on and overtime
Into Eternity.

And, worst of all, you shall believe
Implicitly, in all the jokes, and crutches
By which you'll kid yourself you're not alone
As you were born,
And will, when I decree, eventually, die.
I needn't list the rest. The price is high.

VII

Zeb added, and subtracted (computer-trained,
Of course). It tended, surely, to a minus sum.
He was there, on the dot. No time for hys-
terics. Zeb heard a single voice, shrill,
Wrought up, but recognised, his own:
"To have it all again, just as it was, all mine?
Too bloody right, I will."
(Signed) Zebulon MacSwine.

319

INDEX OF TITLES AND
FIRST LINES